AF207063

Winning Through Failure

The Transformative Power of the Mind

By

C. Robert Banovac

Made For Success Publishing
P.O. Box 1775 Issaquah, WA 98027
www.MadeForSuccess.com

Library of Congress Cataloging-in-Publication data
C. Robert Banovac
        Winning Through Failure
        p. cm.

LCCN: 2024940790
ISBN: 978-1-64146-902-9 (Hardcover)
ISBN: 978-1-64146-877-0 (Audiobook)
ISBN: 978-1-64146-878-7 (eBook)

Printed in the United States of America

For further information, contact Made for Success Publishing,
+1 425 526 6480 or email at service@madeforsuccess.net

Contents

Part II
THE KEYS TO WINNING

To my special partner, Debra, for her love and motivation. To my two sons, Rob and Mike, for their support and insistence that I make this book a reality. To Rob's family: Sheila, Sofia, Nico, and Serena to carry on the tradition. To my brothers Ken and Rocky, partners on this life's journey. To Jen Wathen, and in special memory of Rob Wathen III, whose probing questions about my past during our lengthy evening discussions helped motivate me to write it all down. To all of you, thank you for your love and support in helping me become the man I am today.

FOREWORD

We are deeply impacted by the experiences of our youth. They set the stage for how we look at life as a whole. As we grow and engage with the larger community, we choose our own personal values and desires. We set goals for how we want to live our lives. Each new experience leads us down the path toward who we become.

I am privileged to call Robert Banovac a friend. I have watched him handle huge wins as well as devastating losses, both personally and in the field of real estate development. I greatly admire his unique skill when it comes to analyzing and weighing the risks and rewards of potential endeavors. He is also one of the happiest, most peaceful guys I know.

Robert's life story is full of valuable lessons for anyone wanting to achieve professional and personal success in life. He has proved true the saying that life is not a bed of roses, neither is it full of thorns. Prosperity has both its rewards and its costs. The secret to having a happy life is to come to terms with its ups and downs. Enjoy the peaks, but don't let your ego get in the way. Accept the lows, but don't wallow there.

We can do that by developing a powerful belief in ourselves. Our attitude about how we face life's challenges is more important than our skills, our talents, and our education. Before you can achieve greatness in any endeavor, it's critical that you believe in yourself. Your attitude about your abilities has a greater impact on your results than anything else. Regardless of your profession, the ideas and anecdotes in this book will add value to your life and just might accelerate your own set of wins.

If there's ever a gift worth giving, it's knowledge that enhances life. I believe this book will do that for you.

Tom Hopkins,
Author of *How to Master the Art of Selling*
and *When Buyers Say No*

INTRODUCTION

"It doesn't matter how slowly you go
as *long* as you do not stop."
—Confucius

Persistence and determination are vital for success. Consider this track record, for example, over the course of many years:

- 1816, his family was forced out of their home. He had to work to support them.
- 1818, his mother died.
- 1831, he failed in business.
- 1832, he ran for state legislature and lost; he lost his job; and was denied admittance to law school.
- 1833, he borrowed money from a friend to go into business, but by the end of the year, he was bankrupt. He spent the next seventeen years paying back the debt.
- 1834, he ran for state legislature again and won.
- 1836, he had a total nervous breakdown and spent six months in bed.

- 1838, he tried to become the speaker of the state legislature and lost.
- 1840, he sought to become a state elector and lost.
- 1843, he ran for Congress and lost.
- 1846, he ran for Congress again and won.
- 1848, he ran for re-election and lost.
- 1849, he expected to be named state land officer and was denied.
- 1854, he ran for the US Senate and lost.
- 1856, he sought the Vice-Presidential nomination and lost badly.
- 1858, he ran for the US Senate again and lost.
- 1860, the same man was elected president and became one of the greatest presidents of the United States.

I wanted to begin this book with Abraham Lincoln's failures as an example that after so many defeats, he was able to endure with his positive attitude and not let loss after loss deter him from his goals and objectives as a leader of men. Though I would never compare my success to his level of greatness, his story inspired me to carry on during my own trials. No matter what loss he endured, he never gave up or quit. Instead, each loss fueled his drive to continue toward his future goals. He suffered through major losses and depression and somehow managed to persevere. The man he became was the result of handling these failures and gave him the temerity to maintain a steady course no matter what setbacks he faced.

Abe's past experiences played a significant role in his decision-making processes throughout the Civil War. He would not waiver from his determination to maintain the Union. His humility and respect for his fellow man enabled him to deal with his personal and our country's tragedies and answer his call to greatness.

We all encounter failures, rejection, and losses through-out our lifetimes, for it is a proven part of daily life. How we address these individual setbacks determines our destinies. We must learn to accept and understand that failure can be a building block to prepare us for future opportunities and provide us with tools to manage those opportunities. We must learn to accept and even embrace loss to encourage us to do better next time. Hence, the title of this book.

The funny thing about failure is that it can creep up slowly or hit without notice. It can accelerate and place you in a state of mind where you feel lost, hopeless, defeated, and abandoned, often leading to depression. Depression manifests fear and self-doubt. Believe me when I tell you I have been there several times. Those negative thoughts can block your ability to cope and develop a positive approach to new opportunities. Even worse, negativity is a contagious state. It is easy to transfer your fears and doubts to the minds of others with whom you interact in your personal life or in business.

My goal is to offer tools to navigate your own personal challenges and remove negativity from your mind. This will enable you to develop a positive approach to dealing with whatever adversity may come your way and turn your losses into wins. This book tells my story and how I learned to deal with many personal and financial catastrophes. Three times in my life, I had to start over in business with nothing while coping with three failed marriages. What I have learned from these experiences is that even in the darkest of times, it's our own attitudes and beliefs that allow us to lose or win. Being a winner is more about how you perceive yourself and how you approach life than anything else. These days, I have my priorities in the right place. I am at peace with myself and others while thoroughly enjoying what life has to offer.

At first, I wanted to simply document my life and its lessons for my sons and future generations, hoping they would benefit from my experiences and avoid some of the challenges I have encountered. Based on the input of others whom I greatly respect, it became clear that these lessons might also help others beyond my immediate family. This book will not guarantee you a magical way to earn millions. My goal is to help you and others avoid some potential pitfalls along the path to success by applying the principles and strategies that helped me recover from my own personal and business challenges—many of my own creation. I also hope to help you learn that your biggest failures can bring about your greatest learning. When you can look at all experiences, positive and negative, as opportunities to learn about yourself, your field of business, your relationships, and your business partners, you will gain the confidence to accomplish anything you set your mind to achieve.

It does not matter if your goal is to generate millions of dollars in business deals or to discover how to live a healthy, simple life. It does not matter if you are just starting out in business or have thirty years under your belt. I am confident you can learn something from my life experiences, as covered in these pages. My journey has been a roller coaster ride, and I can honestly state that today I have no regrets. I am grateful for all the lessons I learned and for where I am today. I sincerely hope that your ride is filled with more ups than downs after applying the knowledge within these pages.

Everything in this book is true to the best of my recollection. I have omitted the last names of the individuals referenced to avoid any misunderstandings that might be construed.

Part I

MY STORY

Chapter 1

THE BIG LOSS

"The only true wisdom is in knowing you know nothing."
—Socrates.

It was a cool, bright autumn afternoon as the Beech Jet 400 streaked across the United States skies. Its three occupants were in a state of desperation as the plane headed to the financial capital of the U.S., New York City. It was 2007, and Dan, Ron, and I were riding high as we completed the final pieces of our grandiose plan.

Previously, our company had gained control of six hundred forty acres of prime land around the Glendale, Arizona sports stadium. Prior to this trip, we completed the purchase of Camelback Ranch's hundred-plus acres from the city of Glendale so the city's bond sale would be completed. This enabled the city to build the Los Angeles Dodgers and Chicago White Sox spring training stadiums, which made the area a prime tourist attraction, bringing in millions of dollars annually.

We finished the negotiations with the two owners of the sports teams, putting the final touches on a stadium lease agreement. The owners luxuriated in a large, air-conditioned conference room while the three of us were set up in a stuffy maintenance room. City officials went back and forth as we finalized the terms of the lease. It's an understatement to say they sweated the final deal out of us.

During the previous months, we were able to finalize the remaining pieces to obtain all the entitlements for our assembled properties. The zoning included two thousand five hundred apartments, one million square feet of commercial property, and one hundred acres for industrial aviation around the Glendale airport. We also owned the Glendale private jet terminal, for which we had recently spent $1.5 million on remodeling. The previous year had been spent in numerous negotiations with many interested parties to develop these properties. We were in the process of working our way through a major billion-dollar-plus development.

Added to this gigantic project was an additional two hundred forty-one acres in northeast Phoenix that we'd managed to entitle for three thousand six hundred apartments and homes. We had acquired this property at a public auction from the State of Arizona (at that time, for an all-time record of $138 million). This was becoming one of our most promising deals. We had arranged to sell half of the property to four individual buyers. The close of the escrows was scheduled for December at $110 million. This would have removed $60 million from our debt with the State plus the original $15 million loan to purchase the property. The end result would have left us with $35 million to split three ways. To our dismay, this all disintegrated in a matter of weeks with the sub-prime mortgage crash. Our work over the past three years had us in debt for over $300 million, all with personal guarantees.

So, here we were on a Hail Mary trip to the Big Apple, hoping to find a guardian angel to bail us out. Ron had arranged meetings with four large hedge fund managers who indicated they might be interested in participating in a joint venture to develop our property. Ron had prepared an elaborate presentation, and he was ready for our long-shot effort. He insisted that this was his show, and he wanted to be in charge. This was our first mistake.

We arrived at Teterboro airport around 6 p.m. and had a car waiting to take us into the city. On the way there, Ron pleaded with us to stop at Scores, a high-end strip club. Dan and I had no interest in this idea. We'd come here for a reason, and Scores was not part of our agenda. Ron relentlessly persuaded us to stop for just a short period of time. After Ron begged for half an hour, much to my dismay, Dan relented. It was two against one, and we ended up agreeing to go for one hour. This was our second mistake.

We entered the club, and within thirty minutes, Ron was in the back room with two girls. When the hour was up, Dan and I went into the back room looking for Ron. We found him lounging on a sofa, partially clothed with a magnum of champagne and two strippers hovering over him. It was a sight to forget. We informed Ron it was time to leave, and he begged for another hour. We had already agreed that under no circumstances would we stay any longer. We informed him we would give him ten minutes, and then we would leave without him. He told us to go ahead and leave, and he would catch a cab back to the hotel and see us at breakfast. We waited ten minutes, and he didn't show up. After an angry Dan went back into the club, he returned and told the driver to continue without Ron. This was our third mistake. I had a strong, foreboding feeling that we should have waited him out.

The next morning, Dan and I entered the restaurant at the agreed time for breakfast, and there was no Ron. We called his room several times with no answer. We went up to the room, knocked on his door, and still had no answer. In the meantime, we were being besieged with calls from his girlfriend, who was looking for him as well. He was nowhere to be found.

Ron had the PowerPoint presentation on his computer. Neither Dan nor I were prepared to deliver his presentation at eight o'clock. To make matters worse, we couldn't get help from our office back in Phoenix, as it wouldn't be open for another three hours due to the time difference. We had to appear with absolutely nothing to show these individuals, and we were forced to wing it. Our off-the-cuff pitch didn't go over very well with these young Ivy League MBAs. As we left, we could hear them laughing at the two "yahoo cowboys" from Arizona. I had no one to blame but myself for not being personally prepared and relying on Ron instead. As the former great UCLA basketball coach John Wooden would say, "Failure to prepare is to prepare for failure." This quote is so important. I highly recommend internalizing it.

Our appointment with the next group was at 10 a.m. We still hadn't heard from Ron, and it didn't get any better for us. Once our office in Phoenix opened, we had them forward the materials for our next two meetings set for the following day. We at least had something to prepare with and present. Still, there was no sign of Ron. It was now twenty-four hours of no contact, and his girlfriend was in a frenzy trying to find him. We were reluctant to tell her he disappeared in a strip bar. Dan made the comment that, for Ron's sake, he had better be dead.

The next day, we were better prepared and received some lukewarm responses to our presentation but got no takers. We headed back to the airport but still had no word from Ron. Dan and I were beyond upset with him but also worried. We were on the plane, ready to take off, and guess who showed up? Yep, Ron. As you can imagine, this wasn't a pleasant situation. He explained that he'd left the club with the strippers, took some drugs, and blacked out. Then, they'd stolen ten thousand dollars off his credit card plus all his cash. Dan didn't care and was livid that he left us in the lurch. He jumped all over Ron, yelling at him, saying he wanted nothing more to do with him. Once the screaming subsided, the plane ride back to Arizona was pretty quiet.

During the silence, I reflected on our situation. I felt we were doomed. Bankruptcy loomed. I was in my early sixties, and I would have to start over for the third time. I would lose everything: my seven-thousand-square-foot home on the hill overlooking downtown Phoenix, the Bentley convertible, and the private jet. I didn't know if I had the energy or the will to start over. I would be back at square one.

I learned, once again, that no matter how hard you work and plan, you cannot know the future. Unexpected events can change your life in an instant. It is impossible to control everything. You have to constantly work on developing your mental strength to deal with whatever is thrown at you. Whether you consider it lucky or not, even though this challenge was devastating, I had been there before and resolved to overcome it again.

Lessons Learned:

- When working with partners, bear the weight of responsibility as equally as possible. Even if one has skills that are best used in certain situations, cross-preparation is essential.
- When something big is on the line, staying focused is critical. Business and pleasure may need to be kept separate.
- Always, always, always have a backup plan. Do not wallow in the depths of negativity about what could go wrong, but prepare for the worst-case scenario as best you can.

Chapter 2

THE BEGINNING

"The roots of education are bitter,
but the fruits are sweet."
—Aristotle

In 1907, an eighteen-year-old immigrant stepped off the boat at Ellis Island in New York Harbor. He had just arrived from his arduous journey from the Austrian Empire, eventually to be known as Croatia. Blas Banovac was the youngest son of a large family who could no longer afford to feed him. The brother of the young girl he was engaged to marry had arranged the passage. Louis Habarac had been in the U.S. for three years, working for another Croatian in Watsonville, California. Louis sent his future brother-in-law a train ticket to San Francisco, agreeing to meet him.

Blas was a young man in a strange land and could not speak a word of English. He only had the clothes on his back and carried a dream of building a new life in America. Eventually arriving in Watsonville, young Blas immediately began working for the same farmer as

Louis. It took him two years to secure enough money to pay Louis back and arrange passage for his future bride. Young Sarah eventually arrived, and they were married. The early days were hard, and they both worked to save money to purchase a ten-acre lot with a small home. My father, Charles Banovac, was eventually born to this hard-working couple. It wasn't unusual for young Sarah to wake up early to take care of their home, pack her young child on her back, and head off to work in the fields. Eventually, they had two more children, a boy and a girl. The family of five subsided on a life of hard work, saving every penny so they could acquire more land. My father, being the oldest, was my grandparents' pride and joy. They proceeded to spoil him in every way they could.

My mother's family were also immigrants. Her mother, who was also named Sarah, was from the Austrian Empire, and since she could also speak Croatian, I assume that she came from the same area. My grandfather was from Trieste, Italy, and was full-blooded Italian. He was thirty-two when he married my grandmother, who was a child bride of sixteen at the time. I understand that his surname was originally Benetti, but he changed it to Benich once he arrived in the U.S. to fit in with the Croatians that were inhabiting his eventual destination.

Once married, they immediately left for the U.S. to build a new life. I understand my grandfather could speak

English and Italian. He had worked for the railroad in Italy and immediately found a job as a conductor for the Southern Pacific Railroad and proceeded to raise a family. My mother was the sixth child of eight, and their family of ten lived modestly in a three-room house on a five-acre plot.

Both families were products of the Great Depression, and through their frugal hard work and sacrifices, they were not able to simply survive, but to prosper. My mother's and father's families were headed for a collision course.

When World War II broke out, my father received a farm exemption, but his younger brother was sent overseas. During this period, my father was one of the few available men in town and was having a great time until one fateful night when he met Mary Lou Benich at the Fox Theater. The precocious, blonde beauty swept him off his feet, and they immediately became serious. A few months later, I was conceived in the backseat of a 1940 Buick convertible. Those times afforded very few options for young couples, and the only one available to them was to get married. My father's parents were not happy. It had been my grandfather's dream that my father would marry into another family that had substantial land to further enrich the Banovac family. Alas, that never happened, and throughout my parents' marriage, my father's family did not approve of her. Her saving grace was the fact that she had three sons, and in my grandfather's opinion, "Girls do not matter." He only wanted sons to carry on the family name and legacy.

On November 25, 1944, I came into this world to these two battling immigrant families, which led to a very eclectic childhood. The two families only had one thing in common, and that was a strong work ethic and a dedication to saving money. My grandfather would repeat over and over, "No pink slips and no debt." He was totally averse to the new American way of using credit that evolved after the war.

Throughout this tumultuous marriage, my mother and father were on again and off again, which required me and my brothers to spend quite a bit of time with our grandparents. My father eventually became a non-factor. He had little interest in his family or his children. He looked at us only as a burden. The subsequent result was that my two brothers, Ken and Rocky, and I spent the rest of our lives trying to obtain approval that was not forthcoming from an absent father. Thank goodness our mother was a strong, loving woman who helped make up the void that we experienced without a father figure in our lives.

On my mother's side of the family, I greatly enjoyed the refined Italian gentleman in my grandfather, who introduced us to fine art, architecture, and classical music. I can easily recall Caruso's voice resonating through the house whenever my grandfather was home.

On the other side, it was always time to work. My father's family had few reasons to celebrate, and on occasions when that did happen, fond memories were created. The grape harvest was my favorite. My father's family had a small vineyard, and we would put harvested grapes into large containers. We would dance in the containers, crushing the grapes while my grandfather played the gusle, a Croatian single-stringed instrument. At this time, there would be large barbecues with goat meat. It was quite the celebration. Eventually, he bought a wine press, and that process was no longer a party.

The home-cooked meals by both grandmothers were amazing, unbelievable old country foods that, to this day, are hard to replace. Living with my dad's parents, I learned how to work and keep my "nose to the grindstone." I wish my two sons would have had the opportunity to experience their ways.

My grandparents were barely literate, except for my mother's father, and it's amazing that they managed to accomplish what they did. My father's father passed away, owning two hundred acres of prime Salinas Valley farmland. Only in America was this possible. Unfortunately, my mother's dad passed away in his early sixties. I really wish I had the opportunity to spend more time with him. He was a very interesting man.

Neither of my parents finished school beyond the tenth grade. I was raised in an environment that was averse to any type of schooling, and discussions of higher education did not exist. It was expected that we were to work on the farm, and with time, we would get our dues. As I entered high school, I had absolutely no idea what I was going to do with my life. Education was not in the equation, as my Cs and Ds would attest.

My saving grace was my best friend Bill and his family. His father became my guiding light. I spent so much time with Bill and his family that the idea of getting a college education became ingrained in my head. His father was adamant about the importance of getting an education. I was never interested in attending college until I spent time with Bill and his dad. I did manage to attend a few college football games with them and even toured Stanford University. Bill's dad opened my eyes to new opportunities, exploring the advantages of a college education and what my future could be. I could leave that small town and experience what the rest of the world had to offer.

Having spent my summers working in the fields, I began to realize that farming was not the future I wanted. Yet, enrolling in a four-year institution was not in the cards with my grades. Luckily for me, Santa Cruz County had just opened Cabrillo College, a new community college nearby. It was my first opportunity to start over.

Lessons Learned:

- Your family history does not dictate your future. It's only your starting point.
- Your work ethic is just as important in determining your level of success as your education.
- Be open to the perspectives of others to engender personal growth. Take advantage of opportunities to broaden your horizons.

Chapter 3

SAN FRANCISCO STATE

"If a man neglects education,
he walks lame to the end of his life."
—Plato

All my hard work at community college paid off. I was accepted into San Francisco State University. I had managed to save $700 through my summer jobs, and this enabled me to purchase a 1948 Volkswagen Bug for $100 and pay my first-semester tuition and dormitory cost. I knew that once I arrived in San Francisco, I would have to find a job fast if I wanted to stay in school. My mom, God bless her soul, gave me $20 and said she was sorry she couldn't give me more. I knew she was struggling to get by with my two brothers. My father contributed very little to the cause.

From the time I was ten years old, my mom worked nights at the Pacific Railroad, which meant I had to help take care of my brothers through the day while she slept. We all had to learn to fend for ourselves, and we became able to accomplish whatever needed to be done on a daily basis. From the time I was ten years old, we were pretty much taking care of ourselves. Eventually, we all learned how to cook our favorite foods, and to this day, I look forward to my brother Ken's home-cooked meals with the old country recipes. My mother referred to her fantastic cooking as peasant food. Ken could almost match it.

As I was moving to the big city, my dad offered nothing except his words of wisdom that "school was a waste of time." I kissed my mom and brothers goodbye and headed up the coast highway to San Francisco in the old Volkswagen. Two hours later, I pulled into the dorm parking lot and checked in. I'll never forget my first night in a strange city, not knowing a soul. The self-doubt and fear were overwhelming, and I thought for sure I wasn't going to make it. I had no idea what to expect.

The first week required a lot of adjustments as school wasn't starting until the following week. The second day, I was in line to register for classes, and the young man standing next to me started a conversation. One thing led to another, and he eventually asked me if I needed a job. I responded, "Absolutely!" He indicated that his father owned a bar and they were looking for bartenders. I let him know that I had no experience. They preferred that because they preferred to train their own way. The job would take place on Wednesday,

Friday, and Saturday nights. I jumped at the opportunity and started working two days later.

This job was perfect for me and turned out to be a lucky break because the pay, including tips, was more than I ever hoped for from a part-time job. The bar, Artichoke Joe's, turned out to be a happening place. There was legal poker in the back room and a hot nightclub in the front. It was the best thing I could have fallen into. I was partying in a nightclub and getting paid for it. There were six of us working the bar, and we would alternate as doormen and bartenders. It was a popular college hang-out and offered us an instant social life.

My dorm roommate eventually showed up and turned out to be a pretty cool guy. He was a baseball player. During my last year at Cabrillo, I played on the baseball team and had a great year, but my current goals did not include pursuing a baseball career, even though it was just about every young man's dream back then. He immediately started to recruit me for their team. He told his coach about me, and the coach called my former coach. Once they got the skinny, they both put on the full-court press. I would be lying if I didn't admit they got the old juices flowing. I convinced myself that I could make it work, and off I went to baseball practice. It didn't take long for me to realize that with my science classes and my job, there just wasn't enough time left in the day to play baseball. After two weeks and three strikeouts during a practice game from a young phenom who was later drafted by the San Francisco Giants, I realized my baseball career was not to be. I didn't have the talent to play at that level. So, I threw in the towel and went back to class.

School was a shock. One of my first classes was Physics 1A. I remember looking for the room number, and I went into an auditorium with about four hundred students. I asked if this was the right place and was informed that it was, in fact, my physics class. I came from a school with classes of twenty students into a university with classes of four hundred and an enrollment of twenty thousand. I was not prepared for this many people. I sat there shell-shocked while the instructor went through the grading curve and an explanation of how many would pass and how many would fail. I walked out of the class, stunned. How could I compete with four hundred other students?

I was a science major, which meant for every three hours a week you spent in class, you were expected to also spend three hours in the lab each week. How was I going to study while taking fifteen units? Three science classes meant twenty-four hours a week for labs on top of twenty-four hours a week working. I had made commitments for forty-eight hours a week, plus reading assignments and studying. How was I going to make it? It was a battle to settle into my daily college life during this period. I had virtually no time for extracurricular activities.

During this time, San Francisco State was ground zero for the Vietnam War rebellion. San Francisco was in the midst of the flower child revolution, and we were center stage with the protestors and crazies. We made national news when over a hundred students chained themselves to the administration office desks for days and had to be forcibly removed and arrested. It was wild. I did my best to ignore all these distractions, keep my head down, and move forward toward my goal, which was to enter the medical field.

Back to the physics class, the first test was upon us, and through my fear, I studied like crazy. This would tell the final story. Could I or couldn't I compete? When my grade came in, putting me in the top ten percent, I knew there was nothing that could stop me.

The job at the bar provided me with another opportunity. Several of my coworkers were in a karate class at the university and convinced me to join. I began my karate lessons, eventually becoming a brown belt, one degree below a black belt. This training helped me immensely during my time in the Army, but that is a story for later.

After the first semester, I managed to run into some old classmates from junior college, and we arranged to get an apartment together at Twin Peaks. The four of us rented a furnished two-bedroom apartment with downtown and Bay Bridge views for $200 a month or $50 each. This turned out to be more affordable than the dorm. It worked out great because none of us were party animals, and it was a lot quieter than the noisy dorms.

My job enabled me to meet a lot of interesting people. One of them was Pete. He and I became close friends instantly. Pete attended the University of San Francisco and was from a wealthy Santa Barbara family. He introduced me to many of his wealthy friends, which enabled me to see a whole different way of life, one that included limos, maids, cooks, and chauffeurs. That was something I'd never experienced with my farming background.

I eventually moved into an old house with Pete and his roommate, which was also in Twin Peaks. We all had separate rooms, and life was good. During my fourth year of college, I realized science was not for me. I switched my major to business and got rid of the labs that had been eating up my time. I was definitely destined to be a businessman. Inspired by the lavish lives my new friends led, I felt a growing impatience to carve out my own path to success.

It was time to get my master's degree and charge out into the business world. I enrolled in business school at San Francisco State and was well on my way. Everything was going great until Uncle Sam decided to throw a wrench into the whole thing. I received a greeting letter from the government. I was going to be drafted.

Lessons Learned:

- New experiences help develop self-confidence. They can force you to get out of your shell and meet people no matter how uncomfortable it feels.
- Always be open to new opportunities. When the universe shows them to you, investigate!
- Set goals for at least the next six months to help you keep your eyes open for both expected and unexpected ways of achieving them.

Chapter 4

THE ARMY

"It's not what happens to you,
but how you react to it that matters."
—Epictetus

After classes started, I received a letter from my friendly draft board informing me that my school deferment was canceled, effective immediately. My draft status was listed as 1A, which meant I was immediately available for military service. Straightaway, I hot-footed down to the Santa Cruz County draft board with an appeal. Five brusque old gentlemen told me it was too bad it had taken me four and a half years to graduate when I was only allowed four years. They couldn't care less that I had to work a job while carrying a full load of classes. Once the semester was over, I had to be on my way.

Back in San Francisco, I frantically started researching my options. A six-month stint in the National Guard was impossible because there was a huge waiting list. For weeks, I was in a state of depression. The last thing I wanted was to be drafted into the Army and shipped off to Vietnam.

I finally accepted the fact that this was a reality and started looking into which branch of the service would work best for me. Since I had a college degree, I could enlist and become an officer, but time was running out. Then, a guardian angel popped up in the form of one of my college instructors. He knew an officer in the Army Medical Reserve and suggested that I contact him. As luck would have it, he was on duty that weekend at Letterman Hospital located in San Francisco. He asked me to stop by, and I immediately went to meet him.

We hit it off, and he informed me that they were recruiting new medics for their unit. My education in science was a perfect fit. He walked me over to his commanding officer, and after a short interview, I was invited to join their medical unit. I couldn't sign up fast enough. I would be allowed to finish the semester before I had to report. This was a godsend. My draft board was notified, and I was off to join the Army Medical Reserve.

Once I finished the school term, I left for the Oakland reception station, where I underwent my physicals and received my orders to report to Fort Polk, Louisiana. Other than a short foray across the border into Mexico during spring break, this was the first time I'd left the state of California. Up to this point, my travel experience could be summed up by that one hectic trip when half of my group was arrested in Tijuana for participating in a bar brawl. We'd had to pool all of our funds to bail out two of our friends, and then we had to cut our trip short.

After my anxious flight, thinking we were going down on every little bump, we finally landed in lovely Louisiana and were bussed to Fort Polk. This particular fort was noted for its weather, which was similar to Vietnam. On the first day, we were herded into a large auditorium and given snakebite kits. Then, we proceeded to receive a substantial tutorial on the different poisonous snakes that happened to inhabit the area. I just about had a heart attack right there. Snakes terrified me, and I was now in the snake capital of the United States. How was I going to survive?

Next, we were off to the reception station, where we were assigned our barracks. The sergeant who was working looked at me and said, "Fat man's platoon." While at school, I had been working out religiously, and I'd bumped my weight for my job at the bar, which occasionally required that we extract certain unwelcome individuals from the premises. I weighed two hundred ten pounds, and I was shocked at his assessment. I started complaining about what he'd said to me. He yelled for me to shut up and to "get over there, fatso." Our group had to exercise more, run further, and eat absolutely no starches of any kind. After eight weeks, I was a solid one hundred seventy-eight pounds and felt fitter, but I don't recommend that for a weight loss program.

On my first night in the barracks with forty men, I thought to myself, *There is no way I am going to get any sleep while I am here.* Little did I know that when we finished each day, we'd usually be so exhausted that by the time our heads hit the pillows, we were already asleep.

While we were in formation on one of my first days, the sergeant asked if there was anybody there with a college education. Like a dummy, I raised my hand, and, of course, he put me on latrine duty.

One thing about the Army that totally blew me away was how uneducated the average American was. I was thrown into a mix of people from throughout the U.S. from all walks of life, many of whom could barely read or write. All the educational materials in the Army were written at a fifth-grade level. Coming from college, I didn't realize what an ivory tower I had been living in. I always assumed that average Americans were fairly well-educated, which was not the case. Soon, I realized my college education gave me an edge over many of the others.

Fortunately, before I'd started my eight-week basic training, I had run into a good friend of my best buddy Bill from Cabrillo College. Karl had attended ASU with Bill, and he ended up at Fort Polk two weeks ahead of me. We would meet after our duty sometimes, and he would let me know what to expect, which was really helpful in guiding me to what I should and should not do.

That first week of basic training was lonely, with nothing to do while waiting in the reception area. No form of communication was allowed except to write letters, and a lot of the guys either didn't do it or found it depressing. My business mind recognized an opportunity. I came up with a brilliant idea to buy a Polaroid camera and take photos for the other guys to send with their letters. Every afternoon after we completed our daily drills, I would head over to the reception station and start lining up guys for the photos. This became very profitable for me. Sometimes, I would make fifty to sixty dollars a day just taking photos and charging two dollars per photo when my cost was only twenty-five cents. The foot traffic was nonstop until dark. I would set them up in a bunker, give them my helmet, and take a photo of them pretending to throw a grenade. These photos were selling like hotcakes, and word got around. By the time I finished my duty and went to the reception station, there was usually a line waiting.

After about three weeks of this, the company commander called me into his office and confiscated my camera, telling me I couldn't run a business like that on base. I waited two days and then went back to the PX, bought another camera, and started the whole thing all over again. I figured it was worth the risk.

The Army only paid us once a month. As you might imagine, most of the guys had more mouth than they had money. They burned through their pay fast. Due to my entrepreneurial efforts, I was one of the very few guys that had money all the time. There was a huge opportunity for me to become a lender. I would loan twenty dollars with a twenty-five-dollar payback at payday. I hired the biggest guy in the platoon to help me collect. Every payday, all the soldiers would line up for their cash payment from the Army and then move from the paymaster over to us to make their payback. The Army was becoming very profitable for me.

Our company was split. Half the trainees were from the U.S., and half were from Puerto Rico. None of us got along. Their leader was a former police officer, and he was their boss. They stuck together, and it became them against the rest of us. One day, we were practicing hand-to-hand combat, and this leader had a smaller Puerto Rican as his partner and was beating him up pretty badly. The small guy started to cry, and that really ticked me off. Angrily, I went over and pushed the little guy to the side and told his partner, "Why don't you pick on someone your own size? I volunteer my services." We immediately got into a fight. The sergeants were there in a flash and informed us that this would be continued at 5:30 p.m. with boxing gloves. I was surprised to see over two hundred and fifty soldiers waiting at the parade ground for this fight. I have to admit, I didn't have much fear due to my karate training.

Our two drill sergeants came up to me and whispered that I'd better beat the hell out of this guy; they'd both had enough of his antics. I was surprised by how short the fight actually lasted. My opponent didn't have much training in self-defense. He kept lowering his head and trying to grab me, and that didn't work very well for him. I was able to hit him quite frequently before they eventually called the fight. I was victorious. The only problem was that I'd hit him so hard that I broke my left hand. Now, I had another dilemma. If I couldn't finish my basic training, I would have to start all over. That was the last thing I wanted. Luckily, the sergeants agreed to give me an opportunity to finish with the cast on my left hand. The sergeants also immediately made me the basic trainee platoon sergeant, which is not what I had in mind. The cop and I ended up becoming friends, and everything worked out pretty well in the long run. Things did settle down, and we were all more in sync as a group.

Finally, my stay at Fort Polk was over, and it was time to head to medical training at Fort Sam Houston in San Antonio, Texas. I was looking forward to this six-month program and spending a lot of time in the hospital. During this period of service, I was considering becoming a doctor and I saw this as the perfect opportunity to determine if this career path was the right fit for me.

A few days after I arrived, the company commander called me into his office. I had no idea what to expect. Evidently, he was a boxing enthusiast and happened to coach the Army boxing team. My fighting reputation had preceded my journey. He heard I was a good boxer, and he needed a light heavyweight fighter, which I would qualify for. I told him I had absolutely no interest in joining the boxing team, but he casually informed me that if I didn't join the boxing team, he would make my life miserable during the period I was under his command. The benefits of joining the team included a lot of free time to train, having great meals, and my own private room. So, I walked out of the office as a member of the United States Fifth Army Company boxing team. It worked out pretty well since we only had four matches during my six-month stay, and it turned out to be a fairly leisurely stay. The matches weren't much of anything. The gloves were so large and we wore so much headgear that no one could really do any damage. There were no knockouts.

While enjoying the comforts that came with my unexpected boxing role, I came to a realization—I wasn't cut out to be a doctor. Fort Sam Houston served as a burn center for war victims, where I faced the harsh reality of witnessing patients in agonizing pain. This experience forced me to confront the grim consequences of war and the profound impact of political decisions on the lives of countless individuals.

After I finished my Military Occupational Specialties and medical training, most of my fellow trainees ended up working shifts in the hospital. My captain helped me become an ambulance driver, which turned out to be quite a great job. I spent most of my days sleeping in the ambulance. To this day, I could probably put on an Army green uniform and fall asleep immediately.

Under the radar, I managed to keep my lending business going in San Antonio, and things were going quite nicely. The only hiccup was with my leisurely lifestyle. I managed to put on a few pounds. Our last match was a week before I was discharged. Unfortunately, I did not make my weight class and had to fight as a heavyweight. I did not like this situation. I got a glimpse of my opponent training in the gym. He was six-four and two hundred thirty pounds. He looked like Muhammad Ali's clone. I wanted no part of that. I was getting out, and I did not want to go home looking like I had been hit by a truck. So, I scratched the fight.

In response, my commanding officer was furious with me and decided to make good on his initial threat to ensure my remaining time in his unit was as miserable as possible. I simply leaned in and focused on my imminent "get out of jail date."

The Army afforded me the opportunity to develop my entrepreneurial spirit. I maintained a frugal mentality and chose to spend little to no money and accumulate quite a bit of savings during this period. I had one last chance to take another bite of the apple before I left. I noticed an advertisement by an auto dealership in San Antonio that was offering two hundred dollars for individuals to drive cars from San Antonio to San Jose, California. San Jose was only a thirty-minute drive from my mom's house in Watsonville. I went to the dealership to check out the details. They asked me a few questions, and once they saw my military ID, they were ready to sign me up. After filling out some papers, I was led into the back bay, where three luxury cars were parked. I could choose the one I wanted to drive. The Cadillac convertible caught my eye. I told them I would be happy to hit the road with that golden beauty. They handed me the keys and said that I had exactly four days to deliver the car. I would get one hundred dollars in advance and one hundred dollars when I turned in the car with my receipts for gas. I was instructed not to put the top down under any circumstances. It took me exactly two blocks to break this rule.

I made quite a splash when I returned to the barracks in this new convertible. The car afforded me yet another business opportunity. Many of my fellow bunkmates were leaving for the airport. So, I arranged a shuttle service. I charged them five dollars apiece to drive them to the airport with the top down. Since they were all leaving at different times for different locations, I managed to run three at a time for three days straight. Unfortunately, now I only had one day left to get to San Jose. I wasn't going to make it, so I called the dealership and told them I had an issue with the Army and was leaving then, and I asked them if they could please give me an extension. They weren't happy about it but agreed to it, and I was on my way.

Another Army buddy was heading to San Francisco and agreed to accompany me on the trip. Looking at our map as we were heading out of Texas, we realized that Las Vegas wasn't too far off our route. We immediately decided to hit the town and see what it had to offer. Our Cadillac convertible with Texas plates was well received in Sin City. We overstayed our time there by a few days and arrived in California three days later than the dealership had allowed. As I pulled into my mother's driveway to show her the car before dropping it off, she came out telling me to call the dealership. They were frantically looking for us.

I called to apologize for being late. They were pretty upset and wanted the car back immediately. My mom followed me up to San Jose to drop off the car. They checked every little detail on the vehicle, and we were finally relieved of the car. I couldn't understand what the big deal was at the time.

A few months later, there was a big news story about how the mafia was running a drug ring in San Jose by having unsuspecting soldiers drive the cars from a dealership in Texas to another in San Jose. Unbeknownst to me, I had been one of their mules. I then understood why they wanted the car back so desperately. I had dodged a bullet by not getting caught driving that car.

I must admit that going into the Army, I absolutely expected the worst. Coming out, it ended up being a rewarding experience in many ways. Not only did my time in the service enable me to begin life with a nice nest egg, but it also allowed me to develop a large number of friendships. I had a pocket full of cash, and I was on my way back to the city. A new adventure awaited.

Lessons Learned:

- Develop strong mental discipline to attain greater clarity in navigating life's curveballs and finding solutions.
- Master a range of techniques to safeguard yourself physically, mentally, and emotionally.
- Pay attention to your surroundings, learn to adapt, and seize the opportunities that arise once you understand what you are dealing with.

Chapter 5

UTAH

"In the midst of chaos, there is also opportunity."
—Sun Tzu

Back in San Francisco, I immediately moved in with my old roommate, Pete, in the same house we lived in before. My first order of business was to buy a new Volkswagen Bug. I had so much luck with the other one that I thought I should stick with the same car. I had no desire to go back to school and started to look for another opportunity. Pete introduced me to a friend of his, Gary, a young Stanford MBA graduate who had a commercial real estate company. He had found a thirty-room hotel advertised for sale in the Wall Street Journal for $600,000. It was the Newpark Hotel, located in Park City, Utah. The loan for this hotel was in foreclosure, and it could be acquired simply by assuming the loan. Gary was interested in buying it but needed a partner who would move to Park City, Utah, and run it. Not knowing a thing about the hotel business, I immediately jumped at the opportunity to learn more about the industry and perhaps improve my skiing.

The Newpark Hotel was newly remodeled and needed very little work. It had a bar, steakhouse, and coffee shop, including all the equipment. Gary had previously invested in a steakhouse in Santa Clara and arranged for me to train there for a couple of months. I would learn how to run the restaurant business while he negotiated the deal. While there, I managed to find three employees from the restaurant who were interested in joining me in Park City.

I finished my two months of training, and the deal was done. I packed the Bug and headed to Utah. It was September 1968, and the Wasatch Mountains were beautiful as I cruised through Salt Lake City and made my way up to Park City. We had two weeks to get ready for the start of the ski season. Luckily, one of the girls we hired had done a short stint in the hotel business and helped me set up the front desk. Before we knew it, Thanksgiving weekend was upon us, and we were open for business. We had a full house and were off to a great start.

I decided to cook breakfast myself to save money. I thought, "How hard can it be to cook breakfast?" It turns out it was harder than I expected and a huge mistake on my part. Everything went well for the first few orders, but then we were slammed. I could not keep up with all the orders, and it turned out to be a disaster. Immediately, I started looking for a cook. The next day, I had to fire myself after only a few people showed up and ordered only coffee and toast. Luckily, I was able to find a cook quickly, and I immediately sent out flyers to all of our guests indicating that the old cook was no longer with us, inviting them to return.

Other than those first couple of days, everything went pretty smoothly, considering we were all learning as we went along. The next two weeks were really quiet until we hit the Christmas holidays. Again, we were slammed. Gary and I soon realized we needed more occupancy to make this business work. Short spurts weren't making it a profitable operation.

Working in the hotel business helped me get a glimpse of the local community and its quirks. During the first week in January, a couple was staying in the room above the lobby, and water started dripping down through the lobby ceiling. I immediately went up to the room and knocked on the door. A young student answered in his shorts. His girlfriend was under the sheets. I informed him about the water situation and went into the bathroom to see that they had started the tub but left the water running. They were so excited to get it on that they'd stopped paying attention to what was going on in the bathroom. He apologized profusely, and after he helped me clean up the mess, I told him not to worry about it. They couldn't believe how understanding I was under the circumstances.

The Mormon church was, and still is, a major influence in the state of Utah. They would frown upon a couple checking into a hotel without being married. These college students didn't drink alcohol, smoke, drink Coca-Cola, or dance, but the call of nature was still strong among them. Word spread like wildfire that I was a cool, young guy and didn't really care if you were married. We quickly became a popular getaway spot for Brigham Young University students, and we were booked constantly.

Around that time, my mother was having a problem with my younger brother Rocky and asked if I could take him during the Christmas holidays. She understood that we weren't going to be together for Christmas and she thought it would be a good idea for my brother to spend it with me. Besides, it would give her a break. I agreed, and when he arrived, I put him to work shuttling the van back and forth to the ski area during the day and washing dishes in the evening.

During this period, Utah still enforced "dry" laws, limiting us to serving only beer and wine. However, patrons could bring their own liquor, provided they purchased a "set up" to accompany it. This typically included a glass of ice and a mixer. On New Year's Eve, we closed the restaurant early, and I ventured into the kitchen to offer Rocky a drink from my private stash under the counter. We each had a bourbon and Coke to celebrate the beginning of 1969, before I locked up and headed to a private party.

A few hours into the party, a couple of people came up to me and asked what I was doing at this party when the real happening place was over at our hotel bar. I was stunned to hear this and immediately returned to the hotel to see what was going on. Lo and behold, I walked into the bar, and there was a stranger behind the bar giving everyone free drinks. I asked him what he was doing, and he told me that he had been hired by Rocky, "One of the owners." I told him to leave and started getting everyone out. Eventually, I found my brother passed out in the lobby. So much for me being a positive influence. Upon his recovery two days later, he became one of the most popular people in Park City. He had given one hell of a party on our dime, but never again.

Everything was moving along at the hotel. We were doing well both in the hotel and the bar, but the restaurant was losing money. I learned that a restaurant is one of the most difficult operations to run. Controlling food costs was a beast.

Aside from the restaurant struggles, the other day-to-day operations were going smoothly, and I was able to spend a lot of time on the slopes learning to ski. After a few months of skiing every day with some ski instructor buddies, I became an expert skier and enjoyed every minute of it.

Toward the end of the season, three reserved gentlemen from the Mormon Church reached out. They wanted to meet with me. I came out to greet them in the lobby, and they proceeded to politely inform me that it was time for me to sell the hotel. All the shenanigans we allowed the BYU students were starting to catch up with us. They did not approve of our clientele's activities. Once they made their intentions known, they asked me to bend my head in prayer while they asked the good Lord "to allow this young man to get a good price for this establishment."

I asked around town what this meant, and everyone agreed that this warning was not to be taken lightly. It was time to sell. Gary and I agreed it was time we moved on because, without our student trade, we would have a difficult time making ends meet. We sold, and I returned to San Francisco.

I had a great time in Park City, and in the process, I met a lot of lovely people. I learned a valuable lesson: no matter how smart you think you are, there is no substitute for experience. I'd gone to Utah with a strong sense of self-confidence and came back with plenty of humility. Although I thought there was nothing I couldn't do, I realized that I was not infallible. I now understood that I did not know enough to take over an operation of that magnitude without more experience. I had taken a lot for granted and now knew I needed more knowledge before I would be ready to successfully take on my next endeavor.

Lessons Learned:

- Knowledge is never enough; experience is best, and often, the most exacting teacher. Learning as you go guarantees bigger mistakes compared to hiring individuals with solid skills and experience.
- Not all businesses require the same systems to run profitably; shortcuts typically don't yield the best results.

Chapter 6

STANFORD MBAS

"A good decision is based on knowledge
and not on numbers."
—Plato

I was back in the Bay Area and ready to start my new calling in real estate. Gary had asked me to join his commercial real estate business. His office was located in Palo Alto, so I moved out of the city to be closer to my new job. I found an apartment in a new project near Stanford University and immediately began my real estate classes to obtain my California real estate sales license. It took about three months to get through the classes and pass the test. I was now licensed and ready to go. The office was filled with the youngest and brightest of what Stanford University's MBA program had to offer. It was an exciting time to be in the area, for Silicon Valley was in its infant stages. Apple, Hewlett-Packard, Intel, and Microsoft were percolating in the brains of their young founders.

Gary specialized in apartment syndication. Essentially, he put together partnerships of twenty-five investors to purchase new apartments. These partnerships were mainly devised as a tax avoidance mechanism, providing significant benefits like accelerated depreciation. With this strategy, investors could write off one hundred percent of their initial capital by investing in new apartment projects. This approach made multifamily units very popular, especially among high-income individuals.

My favorite President, Ronald Reagan, eventually eliminated this tax loophole with the 1986 tax reform. Investment deductions were no longer allowed for personal income unless you were in the real estate business. To this day, many real estate developers pay little or no taxes, guys like Donald Trump. Eventually, this tax change, along with bank deregulation, caused one of the greatest real estate crashes and bank collapses of our time.

In no time, I became an analyst at Gary's company and started evaluating the feasibility of potential investments for the firm. This entailed learning comparable rents, proposed expenses, and the estimated internal rate of return on an after-tax investment. Gaining this expertise afforded me the opportunity to make investment presentations and get good at them. I had the opportunity to review a large number of projects that came into our office and make the final determination as to whether a project was viable.

After looking at so many numbers and properties, I became quite good at my job. We had many bright and intelligent minds working together, and with the many hours of brainstorming, that, in turn, became my Stanford MBA. The wealth of information I absorbed during my time there was immensely rewarding. I was honored just to be able to participate and be considered an equal.

I was learning everything I could about the apartment markets. In our marketing process, it was imperative that you knew the answer to every question that might come your way. Your sales tool was your knowledge, and you had to impart this knowledge in such a way that you gave a potential investor a sense of comfort. This, I found over the years, was the one ability that could put you above everyone else.

Too many people get into sales without really knowing all the answers. It is no different than selling a car. If you were to walk into a dealership and encounter a salesperson who knows everything about the car they are selling and how it compares to the competitive models in pricing and features, don't you think that you would have a comfortable feeling about what you are buying? It's the same way with real estate. Know your market and what else is available and how it compares to what you are selling. Your knowledge will put you well ahead of the pack. There are many salespeople in every arena; you must make your clients believe that they are dealing with the best.

After spending so many hours perusing numbers for a year and a half, I concluded that working for someone else was not what I ultimately wanted. It was time for a change. I decided it was time to venture off on my own.

One weekend, I was casually strolling down Bridgeway in Sausalito, and I saw my old buddy, Mike, from San Francisco State. He was cruising the street with the top down on his GTO, checking out the pretty women walking by. Mike was a fellow entrepreneur with a type A personality. I called out to him, and we immediately picked up where we'd left off, even though it had been years since we spent much time together. It was great to catch up, and I accompanied him over to his Sausalito pad and met his roommate, Steve.

Steve and Mike had gone to high school together and had a similar relationship to what I had with my high school buddy, Bill. The three of us became tight friends. Steve and Mike wanted to take a break and were planning a trip to Europe. They asked if I might be interested, and, of course, with my current circumstances, I was in. We planned to buy motorcycles when we got there, cruise the majestic Alps, and have a fantastic time. We made our plans and were ready to head out in September. I left my job and decided that after my European jaunt, I would be ready to conquer the world on my own. I knew just enough to be dangerous! My European adventure was calling. We all purchased our plane tickets, and I told them that I would meet them in Munich for Oktoberfest.

My experience with Gary's company gave me a road map to success in evaluating numbers; however, the prelude to this opportunity also made me realize that there is a lot more to any business transaction than just the numbers. You need to understand the market to ensure that the projected numbers are realistic. It's amazing how I proceeded through life, evaluating projections from numerous sophisticated business individuals who were unrealistic and verging on pure fantasy. Knowledge of what you are about to embark upon is irreplaceable.

Lessons Learned:

- It is possible to earn the equivalent of an MBA in the real world when you surround yourself with bright minds.
- There is a lot more to any business transaction than just the numbers; understanding the market is critical.
- Understanding a project or proposal is one thing; being able to sell it to others is another.

Chapter 7

EUROPE

"Life is unfoldment, and the further we travel the more truth we can comprehend to understand the things that are at our front door and is the best preparation for understanding those that lie beyond."
—Hypatia

I made final arrangements for my trip. My plan was to leave on a nonstop flight from San Francisco to London, spend five days in London, and then head over to Paris for another five days. After my initial ten days of exploring on my own, I was to fly to Munich. Steve and Mike had my itinerary and knew when my flight would be coming into Munich. We all left San Francisco at the same time, heading in different directions. They went directly to Germany to purchase motorcycles and start their journey as I headed for London. Once there, I decided that I wasn't dressed hip enough for the city and went shopping. I purchased black patent leather boots with a zipper on the side, a brown turtleneck sweater, a pair of tight double-knit slacks, and a heavy tan coat. I now had that cool London look that the Beatles influenced. I was also ready for the cold September weather in England.

With my new wardrobe, I was ready to rock 'n' roll and see the sights, which included Big Ben, the Tower of London, Buckingham Palace, and the changing of the guard, along with taking in England's unique pub experiences. I was a total tourist and enjoyed every moment of experiencing places I had only read about. Once in these historical places, I wanted to read as much as I could about their history. With a thirst for knowledge, I began devouring books on the history of Western civilization and touring numerous museums. My experience in London was wonderful, although the food and warm British ale left a lot to be desired. It was time to move on to Paris.

I was in the City of Light, and Paris was amazing. I was given the opportunity to try out my four years of French language from high school and soon regretted not paying better attention in class. The food was far superior to what was available in London, and the architecture commissioned by Napoleon to project the power and glory of France was incredible. I became a big fan of Napoleon and read as much as I could about him and his influence on Parisian culture, as well as the Napoleonic Code. I spent my time admiring French buildings like The Louvre Museum and learned to appreciate French artists and their impressionistic art. I loved immersing myself in Parisian life and taking in the city's many architectural marvels, such as seeing the Eiffel Tower, the Arc de Triomphe, and strolling along the Seine River while admiring the Notre Dame Cathedral. I quickly recognized why Paris is an amazingly romantic city. The next stop was Munich to meet my buddies.

My flight arrived on time, and as I got off the plane, I saw Mike with a huge smile and a wave. I got my suitcase, and off we went. His motorcycle was parked out at the curb. So, holding my suitcase with one hand and holding onto Mike with the other, off we went on one of the most treacherous journeys I've ever made from an airport to a hotel. We headed into Munich in the middle of a rainstorm. Mike hadn't quite mastered driving a motorcycle, and after a few near mishaps, we made it to the hotel. That trip made me realize that there was no way in hell I was going to buy a motorcycle. The romance of cruising through the Alps immediately disappeared. The following day, I went out and purchased another Volkswagen Bug.

I was happy to see my fellow travelers. Plus, Steve's brother, Ken, and another college friend, Huck, joined our group. The five of us were excited and ready to head off on our adventure. We had our travel bible, Frommer's book *How to Travel Europe on $5 a Day*. This book had every tip on where to stay and inexpensive places to get a great meal. This enabled us to feel confident about our trip through the southern Bavarian Alps.

But, before we left, it was Oktoberfest in Munich, and we had to experience one night there, dancing polka and drinking large steins of beer. It was a grand time. Later in the evening, Mike and I were heading back to the hotel when we noticed a sidewalk bar with three pretty ladies sitting on the patio. They asked if we would join them and, of course, we did. They were very friendly, and we bought them drinks. Unfortunately, we didn't realize they were scamming us until several rounds later. The bartender presented us with a bill for two hundred dollars. So much for five dollars a day! It was time to move on.

After converting from German marks to U.S. dollars, we came to the revelation that we didn't have enough money on us. All our money was in traveler's cheques back at the hotel. I told Mike to excuse himself to go to the bathroom and then head out of the bar and hail a cab. I told the bartender to order everyone else another round. The bartender went back to the bar and started making drinks while everyone was chuckling and having a great time. Suddenly, I leaped up from the table and sprinted out the front door. The bartender was hot on my tail as I came around the corner. I couldn't find Mike anywhere. I kept running like crazy through the streets of Munich, having no idea where I was going. Along the way, the bartender picked up a police officer, so now I had a policeman and the bartender chasing me through the streets. The only thing I could think was, "I'm going to end up spending the remainder of my trip in jail." This made me run even faster. As I came around the corner, lucky for me, Mike was there with the cab and held the door open so I could jump in. Mike shouted, "Bano, hop in." I jumped in the cab, and we managed to avoid a major disaster that could have ended our trip abruptly. We both laughed about it, but it made us realize that we had to be more careful as we traveled through these different cities.

We left Munich and then headed for the Bavaria region. On our way, we stopped by the former concentration camp Dachau, which is now a museum. We spent the day on the grounds of the camp. I have to admit it was a life-altering experience. I could never imagine the suffering and horrors these people suffered in those concentration camps. You could feel the death and their ghosts around you. It took days to get over the sadness that lingered. How we, as human beings, can treat each other in that manner, I will never understand.

Years later, I read *Man's Search for Meaning* by Victor E Frankl. It was written by a Holocaust survivor, describing his quest for survival. Visiting these camps makes you appreciate what we have here in our country.

After this stop, we journeyed through the southern Bavarian Alps, passing through Garmisch, Innsbruck, and Kitzbühel before heading back up to Salzburg. It was a spectacular drive with all the fall colors in their splendor. The snowcapped Alps were spectacular. We made the mistake of stopping in a meadow, enjoying the majesty, and having a late picnic. We decided to spend the night in our sleeping bags. Unaware of how low the mountain temperatures could drop during the night, we all ended up in my car with the motor running and the heater full blast to survive the evening.

In Innsbruck, I had one very interesting encounter while I was sharing a room with Steve. When I came back after dinner, Steve was in the room with a girl. I knocked on the door and asked Steve to please open it. I was tired and wanted to go to sleep. For some reason, he kept telling me that he couldn't get the door open. I kept knocking. Eventually, a German gentleman came out of his room and started yelling at me in German. I looked at him and said "yeah, yeah" and turned to the door again, asking Steve to let me in. Again, the German man opened the door and came out, this time holding a ten-inch knife while screaming at me in German. Steve's brother, Ken, came out of his room, yelling, "He's got a knife!" Luckily, there was a chair close by. I managed to hold him off with the chair, similar to what a lion trainer does. Someone must've called the manager because he came running up the stairs. When he saw what was going on, he immediately grabbed the knife from the German, slapped him a couple of times across his face, and told him to go to his room. I couldn't believe how quickly the manager was able to resolve the situation. It took me quite a while to get over the fact that I almost lost my life that night. So much for German hospitality.

Once in Salzburg, we managed to catch a Mozart opera, *Don Giovanni*. This was my first, and it led to many more. My grandfather's love of the opera, which he passed on to me in my early years, led to a lifetime appreciation of the arts that I later passed on to my sons.

After Salzburg, we left for Vienna, where we spent a couple of days. Once in Vienna, we thought it would be a great idea to go to Budapest. So, we went to the consulate and received our visas. They arranged rooms for us, and we thought this would be a great adventure. At this time, Hungary was still behind the Berlin Wall, known as the Iron Curtain, dividing all of Europe between communism and democracy. Because of restrictions, individuals were not allowed to travel across. This would be a wonderful opportunity to see what life was like living in those circumstances.

It was decided that Mike and Steve would take the hydrofoil down the Danube River from Vienna to Budapest. Huck agreed to drive with me and return with the group to Vienna. I wanted to go on to Yugoslavia to see my grandfather's homeland. It was quite stressful getting through customs and entering the country, but we finally arrived at our hotel and were assigned a guide. We were instructed not to go anywhere without our guide. Everyone seemed to be in a drab state and a dark mood. It was a very depressing environment. One night, we managed to find a great restaurant in a castle in the old town of Buda. From there, we looked over the river into the newer city of Pest. The castle was quite a spectacular place with a twenty-six-piece orchestra playing classical music. Our dinner was fantastic and, surprisingly, inexpensive.

After the first set, the conductor came over, sat at our table, and mentioned that he had been educated in the United States at Juilliard and would someday love to go back to the U.S., but unfortunately, it was impossible to obtain a travel visa. Recently, Hungary had been unsuccessful in attempting to leave Soviet control. We could still see destroyed buildings throughout the city and many remaining ones with bullet holes. The conductor asked if we could buy him a drink, and we agreed. After his break, he went back to the band and began with a few words, saying in Hungarian and then in English that he wished to toast "our San Francisco friends." Everyone in the orchestra then raised their drinks to salute us. We realized that we had purchased drinks for everyone in the orchestra, and we were not going to get out of paying for this one. They proceeded to play the song, "I Left My Heart in San Francisco." It was a very emotional moment for all of us sitting at that table. Luckily for us, the cost was very little. It was a wonderful experience for me when, many years later, I was able to return to Budapest with my two grown sons and actually sit at that same table.

Back to our travels: We all agreed to meet back in Florence after our independent travels. So, I was off again on my own as I made my way to Zagreb, Yugoslavia. Crossing the border was again a trying experience. Evidently, when we came across into Hungary, the guards had inadvertently put the visas in the wrong passports. I had Huck's visa, and he had mine. I had no idea what was going on when they put me in a small private room. No one could speak English, so I had to sit there and figure out what was happening. I watched through the window as they literally tore apart my car to see if there was anything stashed inside the vehicle. It took several hours before they found someone who could speak English. That person explained to me that I had the wrong visa. I told them that my friend, who was on his way back to Vienna, must have my visa. They eventually got around to calling the other border where Huck was going through the exact same experience. Eventually, everyone figured out what happened, and we could move on our respective ways.

This trip enabled me to visit both of my grandfathers' places of origin. I went through Zagreb and through Croatia where my dad's father was from, then up to the coast into Trieste where my mom's dad was born. From Trieste, I went over to Venice and then down to Florence. This excursion was not only enlightening, but it gave me a deep appreciation for how lucky we are in the United States. Reflecting on my grandfather's roots, I was struck by the humble beginnings of our family in the village he left behind. Many homes did not have wooden floors, revealing the simplicity and modesty of their living conditions. As Americans, we take so much for granted. It made me wonder where I would be today if my grandfather hadn't had the tenacity and will to leave his homeland when he did.

Once in Italy, I realized how much I loved that country. The food was fantastic, the art amazing, and the buildings were beautiful! The Italians have a fantastic eye for design. Florence was an incredible city, the center of the Renaissance. The Italian masters were incomparable in their art. It's remarkable how much I absorbed of the arts, architecture, and western civilization history in such a short period of time.

After spending a few days in Florence, we all headed to Rome. It was a special experience for me to see the Colosseum, the Forum, Saint Peter's Cathedral, and the

Vatican. *The Rise and Fall of the Roman Empire* became a must-read. One evening, Mike, Steve, and I actually sat in the forum with a bottle of wine, a baguette, cheese, salami, and a copy of Shakespeare's *Julius Caesar*. We were taking turns reading excerpts from the play when two TWA flight attendants approached us. They thought what we were doing was cool and asked if they could join us. They did, and we had a great time.

After Rome, the guys and I broke up again. I left my buddies to make my way to Lisbon, Portugal, for my return flight to San Francisco, and Steve and Mike went back to Austria to go skiing. All this traveling was starting to wear on me. I was getting restless and wanted to get back to San Francisco and start focusing on my future.

The two flight attendants were heading to Madrid. Since I had to pass that way, we became travel mates. We went up the west coast of Italy through Pisa, Genoa, and the Italian Riviera into the French Riviera, Monaco, Nice, Cannes, Marseille, and into Spain. We went through Barcelona and then to Madrid. We stopped at many fabulous places along the way and experienced many lovely times together. I loved Spain. The Prada was wonderful. Once in Madrid, I decided to forget about going on to Lisbon. I sold my car and exchanged my ticket for a flight from Madrid to San Francisco. It had been an amazing trip, creating a lifetime of memories with my dearest friends. To this day, we love to get together and share those treasured times.

This trip greatly expanded my interest in other cultures and taught me to appreciate the beauty of art and architecture. But the one thing that really stood out was the slow pace of the European populace. I learned how to stop and enjoy the beauty the world has to offer. No matter how down I became about future failures, this attitude helped me stop and enjoy the beauty around me and clear my head. This trip also enabled me to realize a childhood dream. As a young teen, I would spend my summers driving a tractor for my dad. Row after row led to a monotonous day, which would lead to daydreaming. I would always dream that I was driving a convertible sports car along the French Riviera with a beautiful woman by my side. Unfortunately, my rows would waver during my dreams. I would catch hell because farmers took pride in plowing perfectly straight rows. Fortunately, I was taken off the tractor, for my rows were an embarrassment. I finally made that drive along the Riviera but in my Volkswagen instead of a sports car.

Lessons Learned:

- In all ventures, do your best to involve someone who will "have your back" should things go sideways.
- No matter how challenging life or business gets, seek out something beautiful in your surroundings to ground you.
- Do the work required to fulfill your dreams. They may not turn out perfectly, yet you may be pleasantly surprised at how they do come true.

Chapter 8

BACK IN SAN FRANCISCO

"The key is to keep company only
with people who uplift you,
whose presence calls forth your best."
—Epictetus

Prior to my return, I didn't have a special person in my life or romantic interests. I was more concerned with learning how to make a lot of money than being involved in a long-term relationship. Upon arrival back in San Francisco, I was ready to change this and settle down. Before I left for my trip, I met a young lady at a party and kept in touch with her during my travels. Once I got back, we reconnected. She was a bright, pretty girl named Lynn. She had a great job and was very secure in her environment. That immediately attracted me to her. We started dating and got serious very quickly. I eventually moved into her apartment on Union Street. At that time, Union Street was a happening place with a lot of hip restaurants and boutiques. It was an exciting area to live in, filled with young people and high energy. After a year together, we decided to get married.

My career goal at the time was to focus on my investment strategy. My short stint in Palo Alto prior to the trip to Europe helped me develop skills for my future direction. I understood how to evaluate investment properties, primarily apartments, that were still in big demand.

Since apartments were still in big demand, I decided to look for apartment sites. I combed through city zoning maps and contacted the owners directly to see if they might be interested in selling their multifamily sites. It took a lot of time and work, but eventually, I did find a couple of sites that I could purchase and resell to make a tidy profit. The fact that my wife had a solid job was extremely helpful. It enabled me to pursue my goals with no financial stress, as I wasn't exactly setting the world on fire. I managed to earn commissions, but I was looking for something more substantial.

One afternoon, as I was strolling down Union Street, I stepped into a small real estate office. The owner, Floyd, started selling me on the advantages of owning property in San Francisco. He owned a few investment properties and explained how profitable they were. I was instantly sold on the idea. He showed me a property he had listed, located on 1911-1913 Green Street, an old Victorian home divided into two flats a block away from our Union Street apartment. The seller would carry the debt, and we only needed $10,000 down on a $70,000 purchase. The seller would charge the going rate on the balance of $60,000, which, at the time, was around ten percent. The rent I'd charge would cover the payment. Since I couldn't put together the big deal I wanted, it was time to set my sights a little lower. I *could* afford to buy small properties, improve them, and sell them for a profit.

My biggest problem was convincing my wife of this plan. She had a huge fear of risk and was not too excited about taking on the debt. It took a while to convince her, but eventually, she came around. We closed on the property and began remodeling. We did a lot of work ourselves, including remodeling the kitchen and bathroom, complete with new countertops, appliances, plumbing, and tile work. After a couple of months of hard work, we moved into the upstairs apartment and rented out the downstairs.

Once that sale was complete, Floyd directed my attention to another property on 2015 Pacific Ave, an old mansion that was abandoned by the Japanese Consulate weeks before the start of World War II. It was quite a spectacular property with great potential to redevelop the home into five apartments. With a purchase price of $250,000 with $40,000 down, this property had terms similar to my current home. However, this price would stretch our savings account. I had to bring my buddy

Steve into this deal. At every opportunity, the three of us worked on the home until the five units were ready to rent. In the end, we sold the property for a very tidy sum of $450,000.

Looking back, I regret that we had to sell that home. Today, I would venture to say the property is worth in excess of $20 million. Back then, it was necessary to sell it for seed capital for other investment opportunities as I had figured out a formula for success in flipping San Francisco homes.

I didn't know much about the San Francisco housing market, but after my introduction to Floyd, I went about learning as much as I could about values and sales. He loaned me his San Francisco multiple listing service book and I studied it religiously. By the time we purchased our first property, I had an excellent understanding of the market.

With an influx of cash, Lynn and I decided to move to Tiburon in Marin County. We were tired of the foul weather and wanted a warmer setting. We found another great duplex on Mar West with downtown city views and a swimming pool. It came with a tenant who was a dentist, and our cost to live there was minimal. We paid $80,000, and because of Lynn's good job, we qualified for a bank loan. That was great, and it enabled me to meet a great mortgage broker, Gino.

Gino not only became a dear friend but when he found out what I was doing with real estate flips, he immediately introduced me to Ernie, who happened to own a Savings and Loan Bank. This was during the times of deregulation when banks and S&Ls could invest bank funds into whatever instruments they chose. Ernie became my banker and partner. We quickly worked out the terms of how he would put up all the money to purchase and remodel my flips. He covered one hundred percent of the financing at ten percent interest, and we split the profits fifty-fifty. I had an open checkbook to do any project that was profitable. We were off to the races.

This was not the area I was planning to get into for the long haul, but it afforded an opportunity that I could not turn down. The people I met and the relationships I developed at that time were responsible for my future success.

Lessons Learned:

- When starting a new endeavor, be willing to lower your sights to at least get started in the direction of your larger goals. Baby steps are still steps in the right direction.
- Be willing to take smart risks. Do the math *and* be willing to bet on yourself.

- Look at every opportunity as a step forward toward your future success. Even if an opportunity isn't in the arena you want to be in, there are lessons to be learned that will likely benefit you in the long term.

Chapter 9

FLIPPING HOMES

"Nothing is enough for the man
to whom enough is too little."
—Epicurus

The year was 1972. I had a solid relationship with Colonial Savings and Loan as well as Ernie's bank book. I immediately put the word out that I was a serious investor and began looking for properties that needed work. Luckily, I found a crew of tradesmen who could do just about any type of work that was necessary. However, we had to stay away from permits. The San Francisco labor unions were extremely powerful, and if they found out we were doing construction work without union help, well, that would have been a major disaster for me. Not only would the cost double, but they had the power to shut us down. We were tiptoeing our way through these buildings, trying to get in and out as quickly as possible.

I accumulated properties in San Francisco and Marin County. Our sweet spot for purchasing was between $35,000 and $45,000, and we refurbished the properties between $7,000 to $10,000. We then sold them for $70,000 to $80,000, with Ernie providing the loans for the new buyers.

Home mortgage rates at this time were right around ten percent. We were rocking and rolling, churning properties all over the city. I remember one building I purchased in the Haight-Ashbury district, which had once been a hippie commune. It was a large property that had literally been destroyed. I couldn't imagine how people lived like that. It took weeks to just clean the place and remodel it into separate apartments.

At the time of the remodel, the Haight Ashbury district was going through a transition. The flower children had moved on, and the hippie era was over. Getting that property into saleable condition was much more expensive than I expected, so the profit margin was low. I learned several lessons there. The whole city was going through a renaissance. Property values were going up, and great deals were starting to disappear.

My last transaction was a beach house on the Great Highway. That building turned out to be a disaster due to all the saltwater damage that had accumulated over the years. I didn't make any money on that one. Sausalito, Tiburon, and Marin County had been extremely profitable areas during that time, but the opportunities were dwindling. It was time to look in a new direction.

I needed to find a new opportunity, and my buddy Gino came through again. He introduced me to Grant, a new construction contractor in Marin County. Grant showed me one of his newly completed homes, and I was instantly impressed. As soon as he told me the cost to build it and the cost of the lot, I realized there could be an excellent opportunity to buy existing lots and sell new homes. My only problem was my pal Ernie was not set up to handle construction loans. I needed a bank, and again, Gino came through. He arranged an introduction with the owner of Redwood Bank, who was extremely interested in providing construction loans for new homes in Marin County. Redwood immediately became my new bank. Their terms were eight percent interest and twenty-five percent of the profit participation.

As it turned out, selling these new construction deals was a lot more profitable than flipping existing properties. I started to turn my interest toward acquiring lots in Marin County and building new spec homes. We were buying lots for $25,000, building homes for $50,000, and selling them for $99,000. These are mind-boggling numbers by today's standards.

The bankers at Redwood were also interested in the Orinda-Lafayette area. So, off I went into Contra Costa County and found my builder, Al. With my first property in Orinda, I bought the lot for $10,000 and spent

$25,000 building the home. It sold for $59,000. I can only imagine what that home is worth today.

Over the next five years, I sold roughly thirty-five homes in Marin and around sixty-five in Orinda-Lafayette. The '70s and '80s were magical times in those cities. The Bay Area was large enough to convey the vibrant urban center for young people moving there to take advantage of its opportunities and small enough to offer tastes of different ethnic societies. It was a wonderful place to be, and I met many fantastic people who are my friends to this day.

I had now set up a machine that cranked out money. I believed I could do nothing wrong. However, no matter how well things went, there was something missing in my life. I had everything that I thought would make me happy. Why was I not happy? I had a tremendous sense of emptiness. As I look back, I now realize that my father's rejection made me think that wealth would give me the recognition I sought. Wealth didn't make things better, and this turmoil made me wonder if I could ever be happy.

Lessons Learned:

- When you find something that works, go all in. Hone your skills until doing that work becomes easy.

- Build a team of professionals you can rely on as resources for meeting new people and learning about new opportunities.
- Constantly watch the market for changes. Try to stay on the front edge of the waves of change.

Chapter 10

ARIZONA

"There is nothing permanent except change."
—Heraclitus

My brother, Rocky, lived in Phoenix, Arizona. After only one year of marriage, he was going through a divorce. My mother called to tell me that he needed my support during this trying time. My contractor, Grant, overheard this conversation and asked if he could go with me, so the two of us traveled to Arizona during mid-June temperatures of 110 degrees. My brother picked us up at the airport. We stopped by his home to drop off our bags and freshen up before we were off to happy hour in the desert. He took us to Bobby McGees, a funky bar full of attractive people in shorts and casual tops, all partying on one-dollar margaritas. Grant and I were amazed by how different this environment was from San Francisco. We both thought this was great. The three of us joined the party and had our share of margaritas. Interestingly, my brother didn't seem too concerned about his divorce.

We ended up having an enjoyable trip, with the highlight being an afternoon at the Arizona Biltmore Hotel. I loved the Frank Lloyd Wright inspired design and the grounds with an adjoining golf course. We happened to stumble into an open house for a small subdivision located on the grounds. A three bedroom, three bath home was going for $69,000. I fell in love with the area and thought this would be a great place for a second home. I immediately put a deposit on the house, knowing I would have to explain this impulsive buy to my wife. As you can imagine, she wasn't too happy about it. However, I ended up selling that home twenty-five years later for $450,000, so it turned out to be a great investment.

I liked Phoenix with its simple lifestyle and warm weather. On my frequent visits to town, I would spend most of my time at the Biltmore Hotel. They had little pool cabanas with phones, and I started using them as my office. I also hired a full-time associate for Phoenix. With grandiose ideas, he talked me into buying a 1962 white Rolls Royce to ferry our out-of-town clients around the city. He then hired an attractive young lady to double as our secretary and driver. On one of my trips, I was surprised to find the secretary answering the phone in a bikini by the pool.

Apartments were still a hot product, so we started buying small properties of twenty to fifty units and flipping them to Bay Area investors. Being picked up at the airport in the Rolls and ferried to my office at the hotel pool was going over big. We couldn't find enough properties to meet the demand. My friends looked forward to their visits and became just as mesmerized with Biltmore and my new resort lifestyle. Now that I had established my presence in Arizona, it was time to find a larger project.

I found an opportunity to build three hundred units behind a shopping mall that was under construction. The Paradise Valley Mall was being developed by Westcor, and I became friends with the principals of the company. We agreed on $600,000 as the purchase price for the land. I hired a local architect to design the plans, and Gosnell Construction agreed to build it for $7,000,000 turnkey, meaning they would complete everything, including the landscaping. With carrying costs, we would be in the whole project for around $8,000,000.

Redwood Bank introduced me to someone in the construction department for Bank of America. One of my San Francisco partners, Jerry, agreed to be my partner in this endeavor. We closed the transaction and started construction.

Halfway through construction, the US economy had a meltdown with the Middle East oil embargo, and in 1976, inflation took off. The Federal Reserve took the interest rate up to eighteen percent. This was a disaster for us since our monthly interest rate was based on prime plus one percent. With our interest hovering around nineteen percent, we were in trouble. We had personally guaranteed this loan.

I was worried sick. I could not sleep at night. The bank contacted us and gave us somewhat of a break by allowing the interest to accrue, knowing full well that we could not afford to complete the project and cover the interest payments. They just wanted the property completed, and then we could discuss what options were available. We eventually finished the property, and to Gosnell's credit, it was on time and on budget. Now was our time of reckoning.

Luckily, a broker friend of mine called and asked if the property would be for sale. He had seen it and thought it was beautiful and highly marketable. I casually told him that everything was for sale. A week later, he called back to say he had a cash offer for the property. He came by and presented me with an offer of $11,000,000 cash to close in sixty days.

As I read the contract, I couldn't believe what I was reading. It was a clean, simple deal. The broker stated this would set a new record for a per-unit purchase in the Phoenix market. I acknowledged his presentation and tried to act as lackadaisical as I could, indicating that I had a partner and would get back to him. I excitedly called my partner to reiterate what had transpired. Talk about a cool customer! Jerry thought we should wait a few days before we responded. We agreed we should not act too excited, or the buyer would smell blood, considering we were in dire straits. We waited three days.

I wanted to counter at $11,200,000. Jerry wanted $11,500,000. I thought we would lose the buyer at that amount and Jerry said, "Let's play it out." So, $11,500,000 it was. We then spent an agonizing week until we heard back. The buyer responded with an offer of $11,400,000. I could not believe that this potential disaster was going to turn out well for us. With this windfall, I no longer had to work.

There was one downside to the deal, though. I now felt that I was infallible. I believed that I could do nothing wrong. My sense of self-worth was off the charts and as such was sending me down the road to destruction. As the saying goes, "Idle hands are the devil's workshop."

The move to Phoenix had required me to be away from my family frequently. The Biltmore Hotel, now my base of operations, allowed me to live a resort lifestyle, so I really enjoyed my time in Arizona. The cold weather in San Francisco was starting to get to me when I was home, but I knew a move to Arizona was impossible. There was no way Lynn would leave her family and her friends in San Francisco. I started to develop a sense of resentment that had absolutely nothing to do with her.

Lessons Learned:

- There are opportunities all around you, no matter where you are. Seek them out wherever you go.
- Pay attention to current events and how they might impact your business plans. Play the "what if" game to think through how you might handle challenges.
- There is always room for negotiation in any deal. You might be surprised by the results you get when you stretch your limited thinking.

Chapter 11

EGO

"Happiness resides not in possessions,
not in gold; happiness resides in the soul."
—Democritus

With the business going well, Lynn and I decided to build our dream home in Tiburon. I found a lot that was part of an existing home and contacted the owner. I asked if he would be interested in selling part of his property. He was, and I agreed to buy the property for $80,000 and go through the process of getting the lot split. It took us a year to get it approved by the county before we could start construction. My buddy, Grant, built the house for us, and the contract was for $220,000. It was a very large home with incredible views of downtown San Francisco and the Golden Gate Bridge. I now had time for new diversions.

A few years earlier, I met Pete Wilson as the mayor of San Diego. Now, he was running for the U.S. Senate. I became actively involved in his northern California campaign. Lynn and I hosted a few events in San Francisco to raise funds for him, which were quite successful. He won the election, and I was invited to numerous meetings and workshops in Washington, D.C.

The power in that city is intoxicating. I began to entertain the idea of entering the political arena. I went as far as to develop a board game called Presidential Campaign, where the players all run for office with the goal of becoming the President. I hired a graphic designer and found a manufacturer to run 20,000 games. Then, I hired a publicist to promote me and the game. I even made it on a few morning television shows and got a small blurb in People Magazine.

Several large department stores ordered the game, and I eventually sold fifteen thousand games. Walking down Fifth Avenue in New York was a sight to behold. Many of my games sat on display with a life-sized statue of Uncle Sam. Even though that diversion was fun, after all our work and promotions, it was time to move on. With the conclusion of the election, my interest had naturally shifted elsewhere.

I decided to make another foray into the restaurant business. One of my favorite restaurants while living in San Francisco was The Cooperage, a hip Union Street establishment. I actually worked there a few times as a fill-in bartender during my college days. Their lease had expired, and they were shutting down. Having learned absolutely nothing from my previous restaurant experience, I managed to talk my buddy Steve into going in with me on a new venture. We decided to open a new seafood restaurant, and we named it Park Place.

Steve knew of a fantastic seafood restaurant in Portland. So, off we went to steal the chef. Once the chef was in place, we remodeled the restaurant, and we were ready to open. The end result was both good and bad. Once we opened the doors, we had a two-hour wait every night; however, we were losing money.

One evening, the two of us were overseeing our successful, packed restaurant, and the good times we imagined in the beginning weren't happening. We realized we were paying too much for every meal. We tried everything to bring our costs under control, but as two absentee owners, it wasn't going to happen. Steve went as far as to state that the best thing that could happen would be for the restaurant to burn down with the chef in it since he was insured for $500,000.

Luckily, fortune shined upon us when a customer came up to us one night and asked if he could buy the restaurant. We were nonchalant when we answered that it was not for sale. He responded that everything was for sale for the right price. After we started negotiations, Steve managed to obtain an early copy of an upcoming newspaper review. Armed with this valuable leverage, we were able to solidify a fixed price in the contract, supplemented by a bonus provision tied to the gross income over the next sixty days leading up to the close. This significantly bolstered our negotiating position and allowed us to fetch a substantially higher price. With the release of a glowing review, we hit it out of the park and emerged from the ordeal unscathed.

Once I moved on, my next-door neighbor in the Biltmore, Paul, asked if I would be interested in being his partner at his new, high-end Chinese restaurant at the Scottsdale Fashion Park. Even though I was impressed with the concept, my past experiences were firmly ingrained in my mind. I chose to pass. The restaurant's concept was to become PF Chang's, which is still, many years later, a very successful business. Obviously, Paul knew a lot more than I did about running a successful restaurant. You cannot win them all.

Back in Tiburon, when our new home was complete, we welcomed a new addition to our family on March 23, 1982, a baby boy we named Rob. Of course, with my giant ego, it was only natural that we named him after me. Things couldn't have been going any better. My only problem was myself. My narcissistic, self-important, giant ego was affecting my relationship with my wife, and it was getting more and more difficult for her to deal with me on a daily basis. She became very angry with my complacent mentality toward our marriage. I let every little thing be an annoyance, and one evening, in a fit of anger, I left the house, telling her that I was out of there.

After spending the night in a nearby motel and cooling off, I came back the next day to find all of my clothes thrown out in the driveway. I casually picked up my things and loaded them in the car. I thought to myself, *I guess I'm really out of there.*

I called my buddy Steve and told him what happened, and he offered me his guest room. He allowed me to stay with him until I decided what to do. Looking back, Lynn did not deserve the treatment I gave her, and this breakup was solely my doing. I can only say that we managed to maintain a great home life for our son, and together, we both now enjoy a wonderful relationship with Rob and his family.

I had my home in Arizona, and off I went to get away from San Francisco. My mother moved to Arizona about this time, which was more reason to be there. My middle brother, Ken, also returned from the service. I was shocked the first time I saw him. He left weighing about one hundred forty pounds and came back six years later at two hundred ten pounds. My mom told me he had been an MP (military police) in Saigon during the Vietnam war, but I found that hard to believe. He had gone through a major metamorphosis, becoming this macho man. He also wanted to spend more time in Phoenix, so it was great having my family around.

I started going back and forth between the two cities. During this time, I met someone in Arizona, which only added to this dysfunctional arrangement. I would come to San Francisco and spend time with my son and then head back to Arizona. In the Bay Area, I would stay with Steve in his Sausalito home. It was very evident that my marriage was over, and with a paramour in the equation, all hope for reconciliation had flown out the window. We began the divorce proceedings, and a very difficult two years followed as we both struggled through this process.

As I'd pivoted from the restaurant scene, I had started building a twelve-unit subdivision in Tiburon and picked out a lot to build a home. Lynn was still in our big house in Tiburon through the divorce, and it was eventually determined that we would sell the home and split the proceeds. The home had increased in value substantially over the last four years and our initial $350,000 investment turned into a $950,000 bonanza. Lynn, of course, got the best attorneys and accountants, which were being paid for through our community property assets.

It is extremely difficult for two people who had spent so much time together to turn against one another. Her anger manifested my anger. My business came to a standstill since we lived in a community property state, and I needed her signature for any and all transactions. Every transaction had to be approved by her attorneys, and it was a nightmare. After a two-year battle, in 1986, the marriage was dissolved.

Prior to my divorce, I considered myself to be a retired, wealthy man. After going through it, I was a beaten man. After all the expenses of the settlement, including selling certain assets and paying the resulting taxes, I was left with forty percent of my net worth. At this point, it did not matter; I firmly believed that I could do it again. Boy, was I in for a rude awakening. I had to go back to work.

The one thing I learned going through this process was to stop and think about the mess I was potentially creating. This situation had a negative impact on my son and Lynn. It took years to overcome the damage. My mental state was not good for any of us. Unfortunately, I carried it forward into the next relationship, and I didn't fare much better in the long run. When you are broken, a new paint job is not going to help. I had numerous issues to deal with, and I was still searching for the magic formula to fix it. That formula was not forthcoming in the direction I was headed. When you are obsessed with goals and you're trying to succeed in the business world, it's easy to avoid pausing to think about whether you are happy. You just keep going to the next goal. Trust me, that is not the way to live your life.

Lessons Learned:

- Power is intoxicating. Learn to rein in your ego when things go well and not let it blind you to how you are treating others.
- Analyze everything! If you are not an expert at some aspect of business, hire someone who is. In order to get information, you need to make better decisions.
- Harmonize life and business goals if you want to be successful in both arenas.

Chapter 12

THE CRASH

"Life is really simple, but we insist on
making it complicated."
—Confucius

The only thing keeping me in San Francisco was my son. I decided it was time to move all my business to Arizona and keep an apartment in San Francisco for when I visited him. Lynn and I sold our two homes in Tiburon, and I moved into an apartment building across from the Fairmont Hotel on Nob Hill.

This arrangement worked well as I went back and forth between Arizona and San Francisco. I kept my place in the city until Rob was able to travel back-and-forth on an airplane by himself. I felt horrible having him shuffled between two homes, but Lynn did a great job of raising him, and even with all this bouncing around, he still managed to become a well-adjusted young man.

Back in Arizona, I was wheeling and dealing with new transactions. My strategy was to buy an existing small apartment complex, fix it up, and flip it to one of my many acquaintances in the Bay Area. It got to be quite an operation as I had my friends coming and going from Arizona as we handled these transactions. I even managed to build a couple of office buildings in a small shopping center. Business was booming.

One evening, I was waiting for a friend at a popular Phoenix restaurant. I could not be seated until he arrived, so I was sitting on a bench when an attractive young lady sat down next to me to wait for her friend as well. We struck up a conversation until our respective parties arrived. They were both thirty minutes late, so that enabled us to have a nice chat. Little did I know at the time that I had just met the woman who would become my second wife.

Beth and I dated for a while, and once my divorce was final, she wanted to get married. I was extremely reluctant to go down that road again, but she was insistent. She even broke up with me for a short period of time and moved to San Francisco. We got back together after six months of separation, and I agreed to the marriage.

I explained to her that I had no idea what was in store for us in the future. She assured me committed couples could work through anything together, even in difficult times. We went off to the Justice of the Peace, where we were married by a judge in his chamber. I would like to say that everything was peaches and cream, but unfor-

tunately, it wasn't. I guess I just didn't learn the first
time. Beth and I were married in 1987, and on June 4,
1989, my second son, Michael, was born. Gradually, my
personal struggles were starting to take their toll, divert-
ing my attention from broader events. As the economy
started to falter, I remained oblivious to the gathering
storm clouds on the horizon.

Bank deregulation offered multiple opportunities that
enabled me to utilize different banks to finance projects
with pretty close to one hundred percent financing. It
was a double-edged sword, for what goes up must come
down with the law of real estate gravity. Reagan's 1986
tax reform led to my demise. Apartment communities
lost their tax advantages. Savings and loan operations
had become wild with their investments, and they took
incredible risks with their development partners. Savings
and loans were giving money to everyone and anyone
who would build an apartment complex.

Now, these properties were overbuilt, and with the
change in tax laws, investors could no longer deduct
their investments in these properties against their ordi-
nary income. This simple tax revision created a massacre.
Values started to plummet. Over-building created a glut
of apartments, and rents were declining.

Every property that I had sold included a note carry-
back. For instance, if I sold a property for $2,500,000

and I had a loan of $1,500,000, the buyer could put a down payment of $500,000 and assume the loan for $1,500,000. I would issue a note for the remaining $500,000 in second position at ten percent interest-only payments for seven years. In essence, this would provide me with $50,000 of income until the note was repaid. I was the signee of the original notes that would now become higher than the value of the property.

Unfortunately, the savings and loan operations were foreclosing, and they all started to fail. The government created the Resolution Trust Company (RTC), which began to take over all of these different properties so the federal government could sell the failed S&Ls. The big banks from California came in to assume the failed banks.

All these properties and assets that were generating my income were now gone. It was unfortunate, but with all my problems, I couldn't see what was right in front of me. The early nineties were one of the most opportune times in the real estate industry. Properties were being sold by the government for fifty cents on the dollar, and if I had taken the time to take my head out of the sand, I could have jumped on an incredible opportunity. I was too busy crying over what I was losing.

In California, if a bank forecloses, they have one of two choices. They can either come after the borrower, or they can take the property. In Arizona, banks have both options. They can take back the property, and they can also come after the borrower. So, now I had all these different loans that were in foreclosure, and the RTC was coming after me. Talk about bad luck.

Once upon a time, there was this young man who could do no wrong and was sitting on top of the world, and now, here he was in the middle of a disaster, completely wiped out.

I was married with a new little baby and going down a deep, dark hole. My wife was not happy about our situation. She had married a guy who she thought was very successful. She had grown accustomed to the accoutrements that came with that marriage. Now, they were disappearing. I told her before we got married that this could happen, but she didn't believe me. Now, faced with this, she didn't want any part of it. I can't really blame her. Who would want to be married to a beaten man who had no desire to get out of bed in the morning? So, there I went again into another divorce. The one advantage for me this time, if you look at it that way, was that there wasn't anything to divide. We had signed a prenuptial agreement, and the divorce was finalized quickly.

Beth found a job, rented her own place, and moved out with Michael. Earlier in the year, we had built a home in the Arizona Biltmore area, and I could no longer make the payments. She and Mike were gone, and as I sat in my home waiting for the inevitable, I was in a state of major depression. I sat around the house all day in my robe, feeling sorry for myself. I was a loser.

This was probably the most depressing time of my life. For the past forty-six years, I had been the golden boy. I was brought up by parents who thought money and success were everything, and I believed that, too. I immediately lost my self-worth and my self-esteem. I felt like I was nothing but a failure and had no idea which direction to turn.

For a short period of time, I went into my hippie phase, growing my hair long and dating women half my age. One evening, I was having dinner with my young son and my then-girlfriend, and a woman came up to my table and commented on what beautiful children I had. That was a wake-up call for me. What was I doing? I was focused on the wrong things once again. I had no business acting like this when I needed to come up with a better way to provide for myself and my sons.

One Sunday morning, my newspaper did not show up, and I immediately became angry, as was frequent in those days. I got out of my robe, got dressed, and went to the 7-Eleven store down the street. It so happened that this 7-Eleven store was right across the street from a Catholic church. I went into the store and bought some donuts and a bottle of orange juice with the newspaper.

As I was leaving, the church bell started ringing, and I noticed people walking into the church for Mass. I sat there for a moment, and I thought that it had been a while since I'd been to church. I reasoned that under my current circumstances, it probably wouldn't be a bad idea to attend. I needed all the help I could get.

I crossed the street and went into the church. Immediately, I realized things had dramatically changed since I had last been there. It had been almost twenty-five years since I'd last set foot in a church. A Franciscan monk, who was the guest priest, delivered a sermon on how much we Americans take for granted. We have so much in this country, and as a missionary, he saw so many starving people or people who were just looking for a drink of clean water. We are so spoiled, and we have so much, yet we appreciate it so little. I realized he was speaking directly to me.

We Americans really don't like change, but circumstances sometimes force us to change. How many times have we been forced to make a change and looked back to realize that it was the best thing that ever happened to us?

The monk finished by telling a story about an old Chinese farmer who had two prized possessions. He had his son and his horse. One day, there was a major storm, and the horse ran away. His neighbors came to him and were lamenting about what bad fortune he had because his horse was now gone. How was he going to harvest his crops without his horse? The old man looked at them and said quietly, "Maybe it's bad, but it could be good."

They left the farm, shaking their heads, saying, "He's crazy. What good could come from losing your horse?" But two weeks later, the horse came back with five wild horses. So, now the man had six horses. Again, his neighbors came over, commenting on what good fortune he had because he now had six horses instead of none. The gods of fortune had shone upon him.

Again, he said, "Well, it could be good, but then again, it could be bad." Again, they walked away, shaking their heads, wondering how he could say such a thing. Two weeks later, while his son was breaking one of the wild horses, he fell off and broke his leg.

The neighbors commented, "Oh, you poor man. How are you going to get anything done without your son?"

The old man looked at them and repeated, "It could be bad, but then again, it could be good." The neighbors were baffled. As it turned out, the local warlord declared war on the neighboring warlord and came to all the farms to conscript the young men, but he couldn't take the farmer's son since he had a broken leg.

The moral of the story is simple. Whatever may seem to be the best thing that ever happened to you could end up being the worst, or the worst thing that ever happened to you could turn out to be the best. So, don't ever give up on anything, no matter how bad it seems, for there will always be opportunities around the corner.

I must admit, I walked out of that church a new man. How could I have become such a fool feeling sorry for myself? This was not the way to solve problems. I had to get up off the floor, take life on, and become the best that I could be all over again. This unpretentious man had instilled in me a new realization as to what I needed in order to succeed in this world: a new perspective. I had to look at my situation as a learning experience and realize that I was no better than anyone else.

There is a parable in the bible that states, in summary, that a farmer had a fig tree that was snarled and bore no fruit. He decided to cut back the tree, and it grew into a large, bountiful tree. I had been cut back down to nothing, and it was time for me to regrow into a new person.

During this period, I began to realize that people could like me for who I was and not for how important I perceived myself to be. I threw out my temper tantrums when things didn't go my way. I saw how much more I could accomplish by treating everyone, no matter who they were, with respect and humility.

Years later, I understood how this period was not only meant to be a learning experience as to who I really was but to also control my reactions when things around me evolved. I had a new sense of calmness without the daily stress of trying to convey to the world that I was a wealthy entrepreneur. Once I developed my new sense of identity, I needed a plan to start over. I needed to utilize my knowledge and experience with the purpose to succeed once again. It was 1993, and time to start over.

I had to draw on every positive experience in my life to dig my way out. All of my earliest fears came rushing back into my head. This forced me to develop mental and physical exercises to help me deal with this overwhelming anxiety. It took time and a great deal of personal improvement for me to get up off the ground, brush myself off, and get back in the saddle again.

Lessons Learned:

- Even when you are winning the game of business, be aware of outside forces that could change the rules and the results you are getting.
- Resilience is the ultimate key to success. It will grow only when you get past wallowing in failure.
- Past failures and fears will hold you back only as long as you let them. Turn them into lessons to move forward.

Chapter 13

THE COMEBACK KID

"What we achieve inwardly will change outer reality."
—Plutarch

The first thing I had to do was get rid of the lawsuits from the Resolution Trust Company that I had hanging over my head. I immediately contacted the three attorneys who were coming after me and asked for a meeting with them together. At the time, I had over five million dollars in debt, and my total assets dropped in value from ten million dollars to below my debt.

At the meeting, I put all my assets on the table, indicating it was everything I had. I did not want to file for bankruptcy. I would rather issue a deed in lieu of facing foreclosure. We all agreed on the dispersal, and I walked out of the room with the lawsuits settled and literally nothing to my name.

Bankruptcy wouldn't have done anyone any good, especially since I was in the business of borrowing money. That would have been the kiss of death. Once that mess was behind me, I had to focus on what I could do to generate income.

The second thing I had to do was find a place to live. I was able to sell the Biltmore home, and my creditors at least allowed me to keep the brokerage commission. It wasn't much, but it was enough to rent a two-bedroom, two-bath apartment. I had some model home furniture stashed in storage from a previous project, and I moved it into the apartment. Going from a luxurious 4,000 sf home to 1,000 sf drab apartment felt like I was circling back to my college days. Now, I found myself in a little apartment, starting from scratch.

With our close proximity, Beth and I were able to share custody. I managed to provide a home for Mike, my youngest son, and I became actively involved in his upbringing. My mother had moved to Arizona a few years earlier, and she was available regularly to help with Mike. She loved having him around, and caring for him gave her purpose. Having him in our daily lives gave us all a great sense of satisfaction.

Coming full circle, I started to look for opportunities in a dead market. I needed to find a vehicle that would offer funds to develop a project. The only things I knew how to build were apartments. The banks were out of the lending business, but the Federal government wasn't. I started spending time in the library studying different programs that were US Department of Housing and Urban Development (HUD)-insured—a loan guaranteed by the Federal Housing Administration (FHA). I eventually stumbled on the 221D4 program—a program established by the government to motivate banks into making loans that they otherwise would not consider. This program offered ninety percent financing plus a ten percent development fee, which was essentially one hundred percent financing, to build apartments. The only requirement was you had to guarantee the completion of the project with a ten percent letter of credit.

I contacted the one mortgage broker who was dealing with FHA loans and asked if they had a 221D4. They did not, but they were willing to approach the local HUD office and ask if they would consider it. We met with the local director, a lovely lady who had never completed a multifamily loan but wanted to work on it. She researched the possibility of this type of loan and ultimately received the go-ahead. The requirement would be a project in a secondary market that had a need for housing since the Phoenix market was overbuilt. We all agreed that Flagstaff, Arizona, met that requirement.

My brother Rocky worked with a real estate broker who had an office in Flagstaff. He knew a guy who developed some land near Northern Arizona University that was zoned for one hundred fifty units and was sitting on the property. I managed to negotiate a one-year option to purchase the property with a deposit check held. Now, I needed an architect who would be willing to wait for his fee after the project closed. The way the market was, many architects were not working, and I found an excellent individual who was willing to speculate on his work.

We had the land and the plans, and we began our process with HUD. We received our letter to proceed with one hundred and fifty units with very little money invested. Now, I had to find an investor who was willing to put up the seed capital to get this project done. I found someone with whom I had done some business in the past, and they stepped up to the plate. We completed the mountains of required paperwork and closed the transaction. It was an unbelievable accomplishment. The HUD office was probably more excited than I was with this accomplishment. We all celebrated, and they indicated that they wanted to do more.

I was the contractor on the job, as I had received my residential license a year earlier. Midway through the project, someone reported that I did not have the correct commercial license for this job. I had thirty days to submit a commercial license or shut down the job. I enrolled in a Contractor School for a two-week crash course and took the test. I needed a grade of seventy to pass, and that is exactly what I got. I received the commercial license just in time. This enabled me to bring the project to a successful conclusion.

Once we successfully completed this first loan, I was besieged with numerous opportunities for new projects. With my new knowledge, I was able to obtain what many viewed as a difficult source of financing, and I was able to find additional projects and investors and build apartments. I put together five additional projects with funding from HUD. I was finally back! I went from being a one-man operation, building one apartment complex, to a company with thirty employees, building five of them. At one time, I had over fifteen hundred units under construction. I became the largest apartment developer in Arizona for a few years.

I had an interesting revelation as my company began to grow. The more apartments we built, the less profitable they became. Hiring all these people and overseeing their work turned out to be a difficult ordeal. I thought having all these projects underway would be extremely profitable, but it was not the same as doing them myself.

Apartment financing was starting to come back, and it became more difficult for me to obtain new sites as others got into the game. I decided to build a housing development of one hundred ten homes. I was building and selling these homes during an inflationary explosion when sales prices and construction costs were going through the roof. I had to presell homes in order to finance the construction. I had buyers flipping the homes at completion for large profits. That didn't work out as well for me. Finally, I decided it was time to go in a different direction.

Lessons Learned:

- Be willing to research ways to create new opportunities.
- A lateral move can lead to something bigger than what you had before.
- Our minds give us the biggest opportunity to accomplish anything we set in motion. Having a positive attitude combined with the power of our brains allows us to come up with ideas to execute our goals to the finish line.

Chapter 14

THE COWGIRL

"By all means marry.
If you get a good wife,
you'll become happy.
If you get a bad one,
you'll become a philosopher."
—Socrates

During my resurgence in 1998, I met the young lady who became my third wife. The romantic part of me had learned nothing, and this was the last thing I needed in my life. But unfortunately, you cannot logically decide what is in the heart.

I had just gotten out of a five-year relationship where we both had commitment issues, not to mention the emotional baggage we were lugging around. I was having dinner one night with one of my partners in a local sushi restaurant, and at the next table sat a beautiful, statuesque blonde woman with one of her friends. We struck up a conversation. The next thing I knew, I was deeply involved. *"T"* was originally from Oklahoma and, as a young girl, a barrel racer. Her father was in the cattle business, and I hate to admit it, but I was smitten. We had a great time together, and then she went into a quiet mode with little or no response. Little did I know that this was a sign of what was to come. After a little over a year of dating, we decided that it would be best if we went in separate directions. I was not in the right state of mind to get married again. However, six months later, she called me out of the blue, and we were back together. My mom was instrumental in this happenstance.

"*T*" was an extremely bright young lady with a dental degree. She also knew the way to my heart was through my mother. My mother loved her, and all she could do was rave about her, subtly pushing me into marriage. This was highly unusual for my mother because her attitude had always been that no woman was good enough for her boys. Now that I was toying with the idea of marriage for the third time, I knew I needed to contact my two old buddies, Mike and Steve. We three amigos had made a pact that the next time any of us were planning to get married, we would have a meeting and discuss it with the others. We had already gone through a few divorces and wanted to make sure that we were fully aware of what we were getting into before we took that step.

I arranged to meet them in a San Francisco restaurant, and as we sat down to dinner, they could sense what this conversation was going to be about. Once I informed them that I was planning to get married again, Steve immediately jumped all over me, going down the list of all the reasons why I shouldn't. Mike was quiet during the conversation, and Steve turned to him and said, "Come on, buddy. Help me out with this. You aren't saying anything." Mike then informed Steve that he was also getting married. Steve sat there in a state of total frustration. In a sarcastic tone, he responded, "That is just great." Now that we were both heading down the aisle, he decided to marry his longtime girlfriend. The irony here is the guy who tried to talk us out of it is still in a successful marriage, while Mike and I ended up in divorce court once again.

"T" and I decided to get married in Positano, Italy—just the two of us. We spent two weeks at the San Pietro Hotel and got married in the little chapel there. Somehow, I knew as I was going through this ceremony, witnessed by the housekeeper and handyman, that this was not one of my brightest ideas.

I was back to being somewhat successful in the apartment building business, and she immediately started on me to buy a cattle ranch in Oklahoma. I really was not thinking in that direction. However, we made a few trips back there and found an opportunity to buy one thousand acres at a public auction. I thought I would appease her and just go to the auction. The property turned out to be such a great deal at $800,000 I could not help myself. So, here I was, the new owner of a thousand-acre cattle ranch. An ex-farmer from California was now a cowboy cattle rancher in Oklahoma. It was a whole new experience for me.

The ranch stretched out as flat as a pancake, covered in grass as far as the eye could see. There were no neighbors in sight, just endless expanses of nothingness. It provided total isolation for my two sons, who were definitely city slickers.

My two sons spent a summer working as cowboys. They didn't agree with me, but I thought it was a wonderful experience for them. They got up at the crack of dawn and worked until after it was dark. I must hand it to them because they were good sports and gave their best efforts to do the best job that they could. They both became quite adept at handling cattle as well as becoming adequate horsemen.

The first two years of our marriage were great. I couldn't ask for a more attentive wife. However, the ranch eventually caused a lot of problems in our marriage. It was not long after this purchase that she started spending more time in Oklahoma and less time with me in Arizona. This was contentious on many fronts.

Somewhere during the third year, she started to go into a deep depression. At one point, she didn't leave the bedroom for almost three months. I became gravely concerned about her well-being. During one bout, the depression became so deep that I took her to the emergency room. The doctors placed her in the hospital for two weeks for tests. During her stay, she was diagnosed with bipolar disorder. She was prescribed several different medications, causing her behavior to become very erratic. I became very concerned for my eleven-year-old son, who was living with us.

During one of our trips to Oklahoma, I witnessed a very disturbing conversation with my wife and her aunt, discussing which one of them was the best liar in the family. I couldn't believe what I was hearing. I realized right there that our relationship was a sham. After a number of years of dealing with her dysfunctions, I decided this was not the relationship for me.

I'm not one to abandon someone in need, but this was above and beyond. Divorce was imminent. When we discussed the topic, she became furious and told me to be prepared for war. A nuclear war. And boy, was she right about that. Shakespeare's words fit this situation perfectly: "Hell truly hath no fury like a woman scorned." We started the process, and things immediately turned for the worse. She broke into my office one evening and took checks from my various accounts, forged my signature, and drained the funds from my business accounts. Luckily, she couldn't access every account, but that was only the beginning.

She and I fought in court for two years. She met with every divorce attorney in Maricopa County so I could not have representation. I had to admit that was a pretty clever move because it became difficult to obtain an attorney to represent me. My real estate attorney knew a gentleman who had retired a year earlier as a successful divorce attorney, and he was willing to take on the case.

"T" and I had a lovely home in Hawaii that we were sharing during this process. On a week allocated for my use, I was planning a vacation in Hawaii with my brother and my two sons. In the meantime, she had managed to obtain a restraining order against me in Hawaii. I had no knowledge she had done this. Luckily for me, one of my partners stopped by the house to make sure it was ready for me. He knocked on the door, and she, thinking it was me, immediately called the police. The police showed up, ready to arrest me. My friend immediately called me to explain what had happened. Unfortunately, I had to cancel my trip. I could only imagine the disaster and embarrassment if I had shown up at the house and been met by the police. Now, we were in the trenches.

Going through this process was probably the worst two years of my life. Every day, I woke up with a big dark cloud hanging over my head. My hands were tied in so many ways. Arizona is a community property state, which means that any business transactions or loans had to be signed by both spouses. That was not going to happen.

It got even worse when she came after me for permanent disability and lifetime spousal maintenance since she claimed that I caused her bipolar disorder through the stress of our marriage. I asked my attorney if this was something that could happen. Turns out it *was* possible. We needed a forensic psychiatrist. My lawyer and I had no idea where we could go with this one. Again, I couldn't believe how I had gotten myself into this mess.

One morning, I was having coffee with my brother, Ken, at our favorite coffee house. This became a weekly event where we had the opportunity to meet a lot of interesting people. One such individual was an elderly retired widower who joined us some mornings. He happened to be sitting at our table when I was explaining this tragic turn of events to my brother. Our tablemate asked us if we knew what he had done before he retired. We answered no. He explained that he was a psychiatrist. As luck would have it, he shared that it just so happened that his best friend, who was a forensic psychiatrist, was going to be visiting him the following month. That man was on the staff of Johns Hopkins University and was known as one of the most renowned forensic psychiatrists in the business. He represented many large companies and states during their Workmen's Compensation trials. He said that if I could get a court order instructing her to meet with his guy, he could arrange it. What a break this was!

We got the sessions ordered by the court. The resulting report said that she was faking her bipolar disorder! As soon as the court received that report, that was pretty much the end of it. She ended up receiving exactly what I had offered her at the very beginning of the process two years previously. We wasted two years of our time and experienced a lot of misery to get this over with.

To make matters worse, my mother died during this time. To this day, I still miss her. It took every ounce of energy I could muster to try to maintain a positive attitude when it was finally over and I could finally get on with my life. At this point, I had three strikes with marriages, and I was out. It would be very difficult for me to walk down that aisle again after this debacle. But hey, I'm a romantic. You never know what lurks around the corner. The cloud was gone, and now I could return to the task at hand, running my company.

During this period, I found myself once again in a major mess that was totally self-created. You can expect the best in people, and unfortunately, sometimes, they will let you down. You have two choices in such circumstances: you either lose faith in others or you continue to look for the best in others. I have met several people who were burned by someone else and never got over it.

They could not trust anyone again. If you feel this way, then you are letting yourself down. You can either be the type of person whose glass is half empty or half full. If you choose half empty, your whole life will be running on empty, and you will never experience the fullness life has to offer. You must maintain a positive approach to others and look for the best they can be. If it does not work out, move on, and eventually, you will not be disappointed, and it will be worth the wait.

Lessons Learned:

- If you get a feeling you're making a bad decision, change course sooner rather than later.
- Beware of investing in something you don't fully understand.
- Keep faith and look for the best in people.

Chapter 15

THE BIG PLAY

"Day by day, what you choose,
what you think and
what you do is who you become."
—Heraclitus

Once I managed to navigate through this dark period, it was time for me to get back to work.

I started working on a large real estate project. It was a two-hundred-forty-one-acre site located at the north end of State Route 51 in Desert Ridge. This property was owned by the State and could only go up for auction if the State could prove there were suitable buyers. My HUD track record gave me that distinction. The State, however, was reluctant to release the property considering the appraised value of $139,000,000. I knew if I could find the required ten percent down plus costs, which was $15,000,000, I could sell off a large portion of the property to several apartment developers who were interested in this location.

The City of Phoenix's master plan indicated that the property could be zoned for 3,600 units, consisting of 3,000 apartments and 600 single-family homes. I had managed to obtain four letters of intent to purchase land for 2,600 units for $110,000,000, subject to obtaining the property at the auction. I also had a commitment letter from HUD to build 400 apartments with a 221D4 loan for our own account. I just had to figure out a way to come up with the $15,000,000.

Not long after my divorce was final, I also received a phone call from my friend Dan. He was a successful businessman in Arizona who had some dealings in real estate. He had been contacted by an acquaintance, Ron, who was working on a large land deal in Glendale, and Dan was on the hunt for a joint venture partner. Dan called and asked if I would be interested in meeting with them. I agreed to check it out.

Ron had an option on a large parcel in Glendale. A portion of the land was designated for the Los Angeles Dodgers and Chicago White Sox's spring training ballpark. The city needed a development partner to purchase the land and donate the twenty acres to the ballpark. Ron had just completed a large project in Glendale and had a good working relationship with the city.

Once in the meeting, we found that Ron had a substantial amount of property around the Arizona Cardinals' NFL stadium that was tied up with options. He also had the city of Glendale giving him a lease option to acquire one hundred acres around their municipal airport, including the private jet facility. He was searching for the capital to make this happen.

During a very long meeting, we all agreed to package the properties together. The total included approximately four hundred acres in Glendale and two hundred forty-one acres in Desert Ridge. So, our new development company now had over six hundred forty-one acres of prime property, not including the one hundred acres around the airport. This had a total value of over $500,000,000. All we needed to make this happen was $110,000,000. We had grand plans but no money. Time was running out. The State land auction was coming up in a few months, and the Glendale land options were coming due shortly thereafter.

We would spend every day in a conference room we named "The War Room," dialing for dollars with little luck. We called everybody and anybody who might be interested in this type of transaction. The Desert Ridge property alone had a huge return with the $13,900,000 investment, and the four solid sales from national development companies would pay $110,000,000 for the 2,800 multifamily unit land.

The State land releases for the property we were selling totaled $60,000,000, leaving $50,000,000 minus the original loan of $15,000,000. The three of us would split

$35,000,000. We were getting close to the end of the line when a representative of Mortgage Limited walked into our office, a hard money lender.

We met with the owner of the company, and after outlining our various cash flow projections, he agreed to fund the full $110,000,000. We couldn't believe our good fortune. We signed the loan documents, and within a week, we were funded and ready to go. He agreed to release the first $15,000,000 once we received the winning auction bid. We had our cashier's check in hand when we won the opening bid, and we were riding high.

Now that we had the property, we immediately converted our letters to firm contracts with ten percent cash deposits. Within six months, we had the property entitled to 3,800 units. Now, all we had to do was wait until December 2008 for the big payoff. Our $110,000,000 loan also enabled us to close the city of Glendale land for the spring training stadium.

We had numerous meetings with different individuals who were interested in acquiring some of the land that we owned. We were making big plans for what we could do with the property. At one time, we were in the process of building the stadium for the US Olympic basketball team. With that on the table, we were getting a lot of publicity. The Super Bowl was held in Glendale that year, and we were able to sign a deal with the NFL to use our property for parking. We managed to get twelve free tickets to the game as well, enabling me to take my two sons to watch the NY Giants pull off a last-minute upset over the Patriots. My two partners sold their tickets for $4,000 each. In my opinion, the memory of attending with my boys was worth much more than that. Our airport jet center also hosted an incredible Super Bowl party.

My oldest son, Rob, was now working with us as we proceeded to move forward with our development plans. Everything was going great until September of 2008. The big crash! The subprime market collapse wiped out every deal we had in the works. All types of financing evaporated before our eyes. We had absolutely no idea where to turn, and our grandiose ideas were going up in smoke. We even went as far as to float an Industrial Development Bond for one billion dollars. The problem was that no one wanted to fund the bond. There was no financing to be had.

Again, we went back to the phone calls, dialing for dollars and looking for a joint venture partner. Just two months earlier we had investors coming out of the woodwork, and now nothing. Our lender, Mortgage Limited, was going through their own problems as default after default began to plague the company.

This is what led to that fateful trip to New York. Ron had acquired some interest from a few New York hedge funds that were considering stepping in as joint venture partners. When we set up the trip, the last thing I wanted to do was take our personal plane to New York because we were getting low on funds, but Ron and Dan insisted on the private flight. Another $30,000 down the drain. I would have been just as happy to take a commercial flight and stay in a relatively inexpensive hotel, but I was outvoted.

After what happened in New York, I knew there was no way we were going to survive. We had signed personal guarantees on loans in excess of $300 million. The party was over. We had no options left. Bankruptcy was looming. I was about to lose everything.

I will never forget the sense of failure I had driving my Bentley into the dealership and just giving them the keys. I immediately put my house up for sale. I was able to sell the home on a short sale. This was much worse than the first go-round. I had no funds other than my $2,000 a month Social Security check. That's as bad as it can get.

My youngest son was finishing his last year in college and was living with me. So, I managed to rent a two-bedroom apartment in North Phoenix for $1,000 a month for us. My girlfriend at the time was living in Los Angeles and came to visit. I will never forget the feeling the two of us had sitting in the kitchen and looking at my surroundings. I was back again in a small 1,000-sf two-bedroom apartment packed full of furniture, belongings salvaged from my 7,000-sf home. For some strange reason, I thought I would save the furniture for the future, but it turned out to be a waste of time and space. I eventually gave it all away. I had to chuckle, for I'd been there before and knew there are always better days ahead if you keep your mind in a positive state.

I had an older Mercedes that was paid for, which the bankruptcy court allowed me to keep. So, I had a place to live and a car to drive. Having gone through this before, I was starting over in my sixties. Despite how bad it seemed, I knew I had to remain positive and keep my mind open for a new opportunity.

I admit, there was a sense of sadness that I had to go through that again; however, at no time did I feel the deep depression and stress that accompanied my previous failures. I actually had a sense of calmness that allowed me to navigate through my troubles. I was able to force out the negativity that overwhelmed me in previous trials.

Lessons Learned:

- Stay flexible regarding the opportunities you are developing. Others may bring ideas that expand them exponentially.

- Enjoy the good times. Create memories with those you love that will outlast any setbacks that may occur.
- Understand that there are always solutions. Acknowledge and be grateful for what you have, and use your positive mindset to build from there.

Chapter 16

AFTER BANKRUPTCY

"No man ever steps in the same river twice,
for it's not the same river and he's not the same man."
—Heraclitus

There I was, sixty-four years old, sitting in my crummy little apartment with my eighteen-year-old son, trying to figure out where I was going from here. I had absolutely no credit whatsoever. When you file bankruptcy, it is the kiss of death as far as borrowing money is concerned. It's amazing how many people abandon you once you go through this process. People you thought were friends want nothing to do with you, ultimately treating you like a leper. Failure truly helps you learn who you really want in your life and who is worthy of your time.

The one good thing about the real estate business is there's always demand for someone with the knowledge and experience to create opportunities. I describe these situations this way: There are two types of people in the business. The first type, metaphorically speaking, is the horse. That is the person who grinds out the deal, gets it done, and executes it to the finish line. Then, you have the riders. These are the individuals with the money who are out searching for horses to make opportunities for them to generate returns. If you are a knowledgeable horse and you can go out and find a deal or an opportunity that can generate cash flow, you can always find a rider.

I like to tell people that they could drop me off in any major city in the United States without a dime and I could find real estate opportunities through the right research. I believe that once I understand what constitutes a good deal and a bad deal in an area, I can always get the money needed for it with absolutely no investment. There are plenty of riders who are looking for deals to invest in. Of course, they will charge you an arm and a leg to borrow the funds, but if the deal is good enough, there would be plenty of profit to absorb the cost.

If you are looking to develop wealth in the real estate business, study past sales, trends, and values. Once you see a good opportunity, you can strike. You can find many individuals on the internet advertising nothing down for the right property. They are everywhere. Don't get me wrong, they're expensive, but if the deal is right, it will work for both of you. Knowledge is the value you bring to the table and get paid for.

I was looking for new opportunities in the Phoenix market. With the housing bubble explosion, the foreclosure rate expanded rapidly. Foreclosures multiplied to four or five hundred per day. Properties were selling for fifty cents on the dollar. The interesting thing about real estate is that it's always trending upward. It will go down in value during challenging economic times, but when the economy strengthens, it will go up higher than it was before the crash.

I found a service that would provide a list of foreclosures and do the bidding on properties. There were also a couple of hard money lenders who were offering one hundred percent financing. They were ready, willing, and able to perform within twenty-four hours of me getting the winning bid. During this period, I met Scott, who not only became my biggest lender, but also developed into a dear friend. He was the individual who introduced me to a wonderful spot in Mexico. I knew within the first few days of being a guest in his beautiful home that this was the place for me and eventually bought a home down the street.

My two lifelong friends, Bill and Steve, stepped up to the plate and provided the seed capital to purchase a large volume. We started researching the various foreclosure lists, paying attention to specific ZIP codes that we knew were good locations and still in demand. The banks were not loaning money, but FHA loans were still available, offering three percent down payments. We just had to make sure that the homes we purchased met the FHA requirements. If we wanted to sell our homes, we could not exceed the price limits. There were still people looking for opportunities to buy a home.

The one thing about residential real estate is everyone needs a place to live. Once I had the money in hand, we started the search process. My eighteen-year-old son, Mike, who was interested in getting his real estate license, started going on viewing runs and researching the houses. My oldest son, Rob, decided to go back to school and get his MBA. He left for UCLA, as he'd had enough of the Arizona market and wanted to go off on his own.

Each day, we looked at various addresses on the foreclosure list that would come out during the evening and picked the ZIP codes that we thought were most desirable. We only had the early morning to drive by the homes prior to the 10 a.m. auctions. We would choose six and try to get as much information as we could in that short time span.

The houses were impossible to get into because people were still living in them. So, essentially, you were buying them sight unseen. In some cases, after a winning bid, we would find the houses had been gutted. Everything had been taken out of the house, including the cabinets, toilets, and anything else that was removable. Some of the houses were literally empty.

These were interesting times because we would see other investors cruising by the houses, trying to gain access. In some areas, it was like Grand Central Station, with people in and out of the houses and neighborhoods. The people going through foreclosure would often have all the blinds drawn and the house locked up tight. They wouldn't let anyone inside. Whatever number we came up with to bid on the house, we had to assume that we were going to have to spend a substantial amount of money to put it back into a sellable condition. This was a major risk since we had no idea what we were dealing with. Another problem was getting the homeowner out of the home. That was probably the most difficult process of all. We tried to avoid the legal process if at all possible. In essence, we were paying cash for keys.

With my soft heart, I was probably the worst guy to send on this assignment. I was continually criticized by my partners for overpaying people to leave. After driving around to look at the houses, we would reconvene at nine o'clock and decide what houses we wanted to bid on and how much we would offer. We were averaging a winning bid on about one house a week, which wasn't bad. Our profit on each house was anywhere from ten thousand to forty thousand dollars, depending on the home. During the first year of doing this, we were able to turn over about fifty homes.

I found my brother, Ken, a condominium in the Biltmore area that he was able to purchase with his VA loan. Mike, my youngest son, eventually purchased a home that he turned into a long-term rental that came from one of our foreclosures. Compared to the start of the year, we were all comfortable.

We did this for about two years. One of our foreclosures was a vacant lot in an area called Clearwater Hills. It was a great price, and since I still had my contractor's license, I figured it was a good time to build a speculative home. I went to one of our lenders, and he agreed to put up all the money with a fifty percent profit participation. I was back in the new construction business after being away for ten years. Back to what I knew best.

Lessons Learned:

- Your knowledge can be more valuable than your skill. Take stock of the knowledge you have gained that can continue to be beneficial to yourself and others.
- Make recovery from tough times a team effort. Combined efforts accelerate success.
- Your mind is the most powerful weapon you possess in dealing with life's challenges.

Chapter 17

QUEEN OF HEARTS

"Do not spoil what you have
by desiring what you have not;
remember what you now have was
once among the things
you only wished for."
—Epicurus

One of my favorite songs is by the Eagles, and it's called "Desperado." I love it because it talks about how the Queen of Hearts is always going to be the best option. After my last failed relationship, I was extremely cautious about getting involved with anyone again. When dating, I would try to determine whether a woman was a giver or a taker. I had no interest in getting involved with anyone who didn't want to contribute to the relationship. I had too much residual heartache from my marriages. I needed someone who could be a true partner and not just look at me as a provider.

Mike and I were still living in a little, inexpensive apartment. One evening, my long-time buddy, Steve, was in town having dinner with an old friend. He asked me to go with him. To be honest, I wasn't in the mood to go out, but I acquiesced. As we were sitting at the bar waiting for his friend to show, I felt a tap on my shoulder. I turned, and there was a woman I had not seen for twenty years. Debra was a friend of my former wife. Little did I know that that tap on the shoulder would change my life. We were immediately caught up in a lengthy conversation. About an hour later, Steve was ready to call it a night as his friend never showed up. I was totally engrossed in my conversation with Debra and was not interested in going anywhere. I must admit, he was a good sport to not complain about me spending time with her, but he wanted to go. I gave him the keys to my car and told him I would take a cab home. Debra and I talked until 2 a.m.

During the next few months, we became close friends. Since she was a talented interior designer, she became involved in the new custom home we were building. She also started to give us input on the homes we were flipping and added style to help us sell them quickly.

I managed to acquire a three-bedroom condo in a high-rise near the Arizona Biltmore and decided to move in. I was also planning a two-week trip to Europe with my two sons at that time. We were headed to Croatia, Vienna, Budapest, and Prague. It was becoming difficult for the three of us to make time for these trips, and we looked forward to it. So, I quickly moved into the condo and left it in disarray. I knew that I would have to deal with it upon my return.

When the trip was over, I was astonished to find the place completely decorated. Debra made it look like a designer's home. What an amazing surprise! That was one of the nicest things anyone had ever done for me. I knew right then and there that this was the woman for me.

This early period introduced me to Debra's strong family values and her dedicated work ethic. She spent many late hours working on our projects to make them as perfect as possible. She continued to encourage me in our endeavors together. Our relationship eventually evolved into so much more. Debra enhanced my life immensely.

We have been together for over eleven years now. Debra has been such a blessing in my life and business. She has outstanding creative ideas. We started to build homes that were well-designed and sold instantly. Once we completed the first custom home and sold it for two million dollars, we started to move away from the foreclosure business. That market was starting to disappear. Instead, we started purchasing small properties and splitting them into lots for custom homes. We decided to move into designing and building modern homes before the craze took off. Debra's designs enabled us to sell our homes quickly for record prices. The last home we completed sold two hours after it hit the market. We've been doing this now for a number of years, and we're comfortable. I'm nowhere near as wealthy as I was in the past, but I have realized that the big house, nice cars, and all the other toys I aspired to own had absolutely no bearing on determining my happiness.

Today, all the trappings are gone. I live a much simpler and happier life. Debra and I built a lovely small home that we both enjoy. So many people think that money is the cure for everything, but it's not. I know many wealthy people who are not happy. I could not be happier with my simple life and Debra as my life partner, my very own "Queen of Hearts."

Our relationship has taught me not to let little annoyances disrupt harmony. In the past, I would allow those things to create resentment and a sense of rejection. As we grow forward together, we are committed to keeping the lines of communication open to allow us to be ourselves while providing strong positive reinforcement to each other.

Lessons Learned:

- Every day, have a goal, however small or large. This will enable you to feel a sense of accomplishment.
- Wake up every morning with gratitude and purpose.

- It's never too late to start a new life, a new career, or a new love. Enjoy every day and appreciate what it has to offer.

Part II

THE KEYS TO WINNING

Chapter 18

LOSS, FAILURE, REJECTION, AND DEPRESSION

"Press on. Nothing in the world can take the place
of persistence. Talent will not. Nothing is more
common than unsuccessful men with talent.
Genius will not; unrewarded genius is almost
a proverb. Education alone will not; the world is full
of educated derelicts. Persistence and
determination alone are omnipotent."
—Calvin Coolidge

From my experience, there is a common denominator for overcoming the losses, failures, rejections, and depression that come with living a life of high achievement. Ray Kroc, the founder of the McDonald's restaurant franchise, hit the nail on the head when he said that "persistence is the key to success." It sure has been in my situation.

I'm sure you have heard over and over again that you should be persistent in life and not give up. When you take several hard hits, being persistent can be the most difficult thing to accomplish. Persistence requires a deep commitment to focus on today and plan for tomorrow. During tough times, the easier path is to wander aimlessly, either physically or mentally, while wallowing in self-pity. When plans go haywire, it is normal to feel rudderless, but giving up is not the answer.

Being called a quitter or even thinking of myself as one simply wasn't in my nature. Remember how my early years were spent learning how to work hard? If I had quit when things were tough, what would have happened to the farm? To the family? It would have been devastating. Somewhere in my youth, I vowed to never quit, and I made a point of instilling that virtue in my sons.

One day, when my youngest son, Mike, was in the fourth grade, his class was scheduled to have a track day. He was assigned a race, and I immediately knew this was going to be trouble. Mike took after my family; he was tall and gangly, not noted for speed. Mike was set to run in the quarter-mile race. As I had feared, he fell way behind and, halfway through, quit the race. I could see the dejection on his face and decided I had to do something about it. I jumped out of the stands, ran over to him, and told him, "Under no uncertain terms are you to quit." Together, we got back on the track, and I ran with him to the finish line. I explained to him that it's important to finish no matter what—even if you aren't going to win.

I've made my share of mistakes, and it's very easy to feel down with failure and rejection. It takes a strong, positive attitude to overcome these emotions. Nothing can take us down harder than constant rejection. It is a fact of life, and it will happen to all of us. The key to living a good life is controlling how you are going to let it affect you. If you dwell on it, then you have accepted defeat. You must snap yourself out of it and start thinking of all the positives that exist in your life. Turn yourself into an achiever with a strong new perspective. It won't always be easy to do, but with persistence, you will turn things around.

During my first go-round down to the bottom, it took a church sermon to knock out the negativity that I was allowing to handcuff me to that low point. By the time I reached this point, I had let myself go in many ways. A lot of people eat and drink their way through depression, and I was no different. Being overweight and lying around the house, I had no energy to do anything. I did not care how I looked, nor did I care to see anyone. No wonder my wife left. I would have left me, too. It took the sermon I mentioned in Chapter 12 to put me back on track toward a positive state of mind.

I gained a clear understanding that I was the only person with the key to change. I had to make changes in my life and, most importantly, my perspective to get back on track. I had to start from the very beginning and focus on myself before I could begin to work toward a successful life. I had to stay positive and force my way in a direction where I could obtain my positive objectives.

As you have read, my list of failures has been long. However, I can't imagine anyone with a desire to achieve great things going through life and not failing at one or even many things. That is just the nature of what we deal with every day.

As a former baseball player, I remember striking out once or twice but always going back up that third time, thinking, "I am not going to make the same mistakes I made the last time. I am going to get this hit." Sports are a great imitation of life. You will fail, but it's the individual who learns from those failures and tries again that becomes the winner. You can't let fear of failure paralyze you.

Paralysis, brought about by giving in to fear, can be deadly. At least, it can destroy any opportunity you may have to succeed. At worst, you might give up altogether, not even wanting to live. Learn to approach each failure as a learning experience. Evaluate what went wrong and what can be done to create a new opportunity or a new approach to the old one. When you hang on to fear, you prolong a stressful state of mind, which leads nowhere.

My dear friend, Tom Hopkins, a very successful author who has published many books on the art of selling, specializes in turning no's to yeses. He does this through positive reinforcement in a belief that you can and will succeed.

One of his favorite stories to tell is how he got his real estate career going. He had been in the business for six months and had made only one sale. He complained about this to his office manager, who suggested they go for a ride in his new car. Tom was enjoying the beautiful Southern California weather and the great ride in the beautiful car. The manager drove into a nice neighborhood and stopped. He told Tom to get out of the car and knock on doors all the way back to the office. Tom was appalled. That was the last thing he wanted to do. They had to be well over a mile from the office. He was told the odds were that one out of one hundred homeowners there would want to buy or sell real estate. Then, his manager drove off. As you can imagine, Tom wasn't happy knowing he had to walk back to the office. He decided he'd prove the manager wrong and started knocking on doors and counting.

Tom realized he wasn't very good at this and tried different greetings. He started to refine his presentation to find ways he could connect with each homeowner who answered. He wanted to be a successful agent and knew he had no choice but to continue. He started thinking that if the manager was right, then each no was bringing him closer to a yes. It was pretty far into the walk back to the office, but he did encounter a couple who had decided the night before that they needed to sell their home. They didn't know any real estate agents, and the next thing they knew, Tom was at their door. Tom took the listing, and his change in perspective helped him launch what became a record-breaking career.

Tom learned two valuable lessons that day. The first was to not allow the no's to discourage him. The second was to continuously refine his presentation to achieve his goal. He became extremely successful as a lecturer on the keys to a successful career in sales. I highly recommend his books as guides for eliminating your fear of rejection and developing a positive attitude.

We all fear failure. We all worry about the "what ifs" of life. Once you experience failure and manage to overcome it, it helps remove this fear and eliminates the roadblocks preventing you from moving forward to accomplish your goals. In a sense, you realize you haven't really failed but rather learned a valuable lesson that enables you to savor your success. My first major failure was devastating, but once I got over it, I never worried about whether I would succeed or fail; I only focused on my goals. Franklin D. Roosevelt once said, "The only fear we have is fear itself." Remove that fear and let nothing interfere with your life goals.

You cannot let rejection stop you from pursuing your goals. Learn from those no's and press on. In the following chapters, we'll discuss the keys to a successful life. It took me many years of ups and downs to understand my inner self, and if I can pass on what I learned, hopefully, it can be beneficial to you as well.

Lessons Learned:

- No matter how hard the hit, dwell on the lessons you learned instead of the damage done.
- When you exercise persistence, you stack the odds of success in your favor.
- Accept that failure is a natural part of reaching for great success. Do not let it kill your desire.

Chapter 19

HEALTH

"When health is absent, wisdom cannot reveal itself,
strength cannot fight, intelligence cannot be applied,
art cannot become manifest,
wealth becomes useless."
—Herophilus

Let me begin this chapter by saying I'm not a doctor, and I don't know your specific health needs. Our health is something very personal to each of us and something that we must learn to deal with on our own. There are so many books and approaches to weight loss; I cannot say which will work for you. What I'm sharing here is what worked for me.

During my lowest period, my first objective was to get myself healthy again. Before the real estate crash, I made a point of taking care of myself with a daily five-mile run and managed to get to the gym three times a week. This schedule came to a screeching halt when the crash happened. I was too stressed and depressed to move. Up to that point in time, I hadn't seen too many curveballs. I was now overwhelmed with them. I was not prepared to take on those daily challenges. I was in no condition, mentally, to cope with these stressful situations because I was not at my best. I was a mess and could not shake feeling sorry for myself.

My failure at that time was not entirely my fault, so it was easy to put the blame elsewhere. However, the bottom line was that everything within my sphere was a product of self-creation. When I eventually woke up to that reality, I realized I had to become the best version of myself that I could be. I wasn't going to accomplish anything in my current state. I had to get my personal state back in order first.

I had to persistently remind myself that a strong body helps create a strong mind. My number one goal was to cut back on drinking. I had become a bloated slob, and I needed to lose weight. I'm sure you've heard the saying, "You are what you eat." Well, I wasn't eating well and didn't like who I had become.

My goal at that time was pretty simple: just eat less. Sometimes, it takes a while for our brains to catch up with our stomachs. Our stomachs can be full enough, but our brains might still send hunger signals. How many times have you sat down at a table, eaten a lot of food, and min-utes later suddenly felt stuffed? I hadn't even noticed how much I was eating, and it was high time I did.

I chose to eat less and more slowly, thus savoring every bite. I found this to be extremely satisfying. Being "present" at my meals, I realized I could eat less and still feel satisfied. I also started to drink a glass of water before each meal. This sort of primed the pump, if you will, to make me feel full sooner. If nothing else, this enabled me to lose weight without changing my diet. Instead of three slices of pizza, I would eat two and feel satisfied. My former "whole bag" of French fries became enough when I only ate half, and so on and so forth. By doing this, I cut my calorie intake back dramatically. In a month, I lost twelve pounds. I felt better physically and mentally. I was achieving success in at least one area of my life.

If you pay any attention at all to the media when it comes to health, you probably already know there is a lot of food you should stay away from. A diet heavy on sugar is not going to help you. Salt is another culprit. Most processed foods are packed with both. Pay attention to that and eat them sparingly.

A lot of starches aren't good for you either. Again, I am not saying not to eat *any* of these items; otherwise, your body will crave them more intensely, but eat them sparingly. Instead, try to eat as many vegetables as possible. They are full of fiber and antioxidants. When you want to snack, try to go for healthy options such as fruit, cheese, or nuts.

Carrying too much weight will make you feel tired. This negatively impacts your ability to achieve your goals. Losing a few pounds will not only make you feel better physically, but it will also make you feel a lot better *about yourself.* I realize not everyone needs to lose weight, but consuming the right foods in the right quantities goes a long way toward putting us all in a stronger frame of mind.

Having good health also requires exercise. I am not trying to convince you to run out, join a gym, and start working out every day. A lot of people just don't have the desire or energy to work out. I was at that point. I had no interest in jogging again. That requires dedication and commitment. At my lowest point, there was no way I could mentally convince myself to do it. Jogging is a wonderful form of exercise, but there are other simple ways to accomplish what you need. Just move your body any way you can.

Walking is one of the healthiest things you can do to prolong your life. While you're walking, focus on your breath. Something as simple as breathing techniques can enhance your physical health and lower stress. Proper breathing improves oxygen levels and clears the mind. If you get depressed, go for a long walk. You will be surprised at how much better you will feel when you get back. In several European countries, it's common to take a gentle walk after dinner. Even walking for two to three minutes after each meal helps you to digest your food.

It also gets your blood circulating and contributes to weight loss. For me, it was to breathe in while counting to five and counting again while exhaling.

Most of our phones these days have step counters. Start tracking your steps and try to do a little more each day. Some experts recommend at least five thousand steps a day for health. These days, the first thing I do each morning is walk around the house for about five minutes. That alone allows me to start my day with about five hundred steps. Then, I eat my breakfast and I walk around for another three minutes. That gives me another three hundred steps. By the time I leave the house, I've walked close to one thousand steps, which is a nice start to the day.

To get more steps in your day, I suggest you make small changes to your daily activities. For example, you can park at the outer edges of parking lots. When I head to the grocery store, I'll walk a couple of laps around the store before I start my actual shopping. There are all kinds of little tricks to get five thousand steps or more each day without going to a gym.

Here's another idea. If you don't like walking, dance. Yes, you read that correctly, dance. Pick three of your favorite songs and dance to them three times a day. It's great exercise. If you're really energetic, shadow box with an imaginary Mohammed Ali for a couple of rounds. Just keep moving. You will be amazed by how you feel at the end of the day.

It's not healthy for us to lay around or sit in front of a computer all day. By incorporating these simple things, it will make a huge difference in how you feel. Moving more and eating healthy will help you to become who you want to be.

This simple program helped me immensely. After the first month, I began to feel like my old self. I had more energy, and I was ready to tackle each goal I set for the day. The hardest part was getting started. You might not feel like doing anything, but you must force your body to move.

Health experts also often recommend multivitamins to supplement our diets. Many of the foods we eat provide less than our daily needs of vitamins and minerals. Our bodies crave proper nutrition and respond amazingly when they get it.

Once you start taking better care of yourself, you'll be surprised by how your endorphins kick in and how much better you will feel about yourself, both mentally and physically. Your sleep will likely improve as well.

Sleep is an extremely important component of health and well-being. Good sleep is mandatory to allow your body to regenerate and your mind to recharge. Establishing and maintaining a regular sleep pattern can work wonders. Try to go to bed close to the same time every evening. There will be times, of course, when you will break this rule, but try not to make a habit of it. How can you soar with the eagles in the morning when you are out with the owls at night?

I have found that it is helpful to avoid eating right before going to bed. All this does is create physical discomfort, and your body is likely to struggle to digest the food properly. Current advice tells us it's best to wait three hours after a meal before you settle down for bed. Avoiding electronics at least ten minutes prior to sleep is helpful, too. All they do is put your brain in alert mode and make it more difficult for you to fall asleep. Instead, I recommend reading a physical book. This accomplishes two things: The first is to take your mind off whatever your concerns were during the day. The second is that it will help put your mind in a relaxed state, enabling you to fall asleep more easily. Six to eight hours of sleep a night is recommended but not necessarily required. Every one of us is different and may require more or less sleeping time.

Another important aspect of health I want to address is alcohol. It's easy to try to drown your sorrows with alcohol. We all have our personal preferences regarding alcohol. All I can say health-wise is that experts recommend no more than one drink a day for women and two drinks per day for men. Occasionally, going over that limit will not hurt you in the long run, but when over-indulging happens often, you risk all kinds of health issues. Alcohol is a depressant, and it is a proven fact that it disrupts the function of our brain cells. It clouds our thinking and eliminates our ability to focus on what is really important in our lives.

For people who drink to escape reality and hide from their depression and the stress of daily life, alcohol is extremely dangerous. I have seen too many successful men fall into that rabbit hole after experiencing a loss. Throughout my life, I watched dear friends give up and succumb to alcoholism. It is a dead-end street, and once you slip into it, it is extremely difficult to escape. If you find yourself heading down this road, please seek help and make every effort to turn yourself around and get back into enjoying what gifts you have to offer the world. Recovery is possible.

There was a time in my life when I liked to party with the best of them and deal with the consequences the morning after, but I can assure you, nothing positive ever came from those excursions. If you are seeking a rewarding life, I can only emphasize drinking moderately or not at all.

You will be surprised by how much better you feel about yourself when you implement this simple program and develop a daily routine focused on health. It helped me immensely to maintain a positive approach to the many failures and challenges in my life.

You must take care of yourself first and be strong in body and mind before you go out into the world and be of value to anyone else. Success starts with you and how you feel about yourself. Building your self-confidence is essential to deal with anything coming your way.

Lessons Learned:

- The state of your physical body impacts the state of your attitude.
- Even small changes in physical health can make a tremendous positive impact on your mental health.
- Be mindful of your escape dependencies when you are low so you can moderate them.

Chapter 20

ATTITUDE

"It is during our darkest times
that we must focus to see the light."
—Aristotle

Developing a positive attitude is one of the best things I've ever done for myself and for those around me. It has given me strength and the presence of mind to gain perspective on both challenges and successes. Plus, it has led to a practice of gratitude. It was my negative attitude about my life's experiences that allowed me to sink into those deep, dark depressions during times of loss, and my positive attitude brought me out of those times.

One of my favorite motivational authors is Harvey Mackay, and he states, "I have never met a successful pessimist." It's easy to fall into pessimism when you experience business setbacks or failures and when your relationships fall apart. The trick is not to allow yourself to stay there.

No matter how competent you are, the mind can convince you that you are incompetent or unworthy, especially when facing tough situations. Self-doubt and self-pity are powerful influences when you let them have free rein over your attitude. They can easily lead to frustration, anger, and depression.

During my toughest times, I allowed frustration and anger into too many interactions with others. I had what you'd call a "short fuse." Even the smallest of frustrations or inconveniences would set me off. It took quite a while for me to realize the damage my anger was causing to my relationships. Who wants to do business with or be married to someone who gets angry at the littlest things?

That wonderful church sermon about how good we have it as Americans is what snapped me out of the false reality I had created. Sure, I had a run of pretty bad experiences, many of which were beyond my control. However, I realized I did have control over something, even at that lowest point. I could control my attitude.

Without a doubt, overcoming negativity is one of the most difficult aspects of self-realization and self-management. We all learn to fear failure, rejection, and depression. The key to overcoming them is to enhance our desire for resilience and persistence and to have a firm belief in ourselves. Coming to terms with the fact that life won't be filled with all things positive and successful can be a rude awakening, but once managed, it can lead to a much more satisfying life.

I'm reminded of the story of an old farmer who, at ninety years of age, was asked how he had remained so positive, determined, and cheerful throughout life. After all, he'd experienced a lot of tough times in the Dust Bowl, with years of scorching heat, flooding, failed crops, and banks foreclosing on surrounding farms. His friends and family pressed him for the secret to his continued optimism. He answered with a twinkle in his eye, "It isn't so hard. I learned to cooperate with the inevitable. Our minds are like gardens. Each day, we have to weed out the negativity." The concept of weeding out negativity as a daily practice stuck with me when I heard that story. I became hyper-conscious of when and how negativity was impacting me and worked hard to counteract it. My new goal in life became to live happily—no matter what.

It's normal to have some regrets in life. That's because every opportunity affords us at least two paths, which can easily lead us to question the "what ifs." What if we had taken that other path? What if we had said "no" to that decision? What if we had pursued this, that, or the other thing? The secret to winning more in life is to reduce the number of "what ifs" we cling to. Our attitudes play a huge role in this.

Forbes magazine featured an article by Eric Jackson titled "The 25 Biggest Regrets in Life." These are some highlights that resonate most with me from this list:

1. Working so much at the expense of family and friends
2. Not staying in touch with friends from childhood
3. Losing my true love
4. Not having enough confidence in myself
5. Not applying for the dream job
6. Being happier and not taking life so seriously
7. Not going on more trips with family and friends
8. Letting my marriage break down
9. Not spending more time with my kids
10. Not being a better father or mother

There is one thing all of these regrets have in common. Every one of these regrets stems from the recognition that the results of the actions are the fault of the doer. I want to emphasize to you how important it is to take positive action in your life when opportunities present themselves. Your actions are dependent upon your attitude. Re-read the list above and consider your attitude about each. To turn each of those regrets into something positive requires, first, an acknowledgment that you have that regret and, second, a desire to address it. You can only address it by changing your attitude about it. Then and only then will you take the actions necessary to correct or avoid those situations. The entire purpose of this book is to inspire you to take control of your attitude and to take the positive actions necessary to succeed.

So, how do we take control of our attitude? Here are some methods I rely on:

1. Practice gratitude. Unless you are naked, hungry, sick, and lying in a garbage heap in horrendous weather, you have something to be grateful for. Look around you now at five things you are currently grateful for, such as a roof over your head, shoes on your feet, food in your refrigerator, loved ones, good eyesight to read this information, and a mind that seeks to learn new things. Notice how your spirit lifts when you experience gratitude. It practically sweeps away negativity.

2. Savor pleasure. We are good at experiencing pleasure at special events and parties, but try to focus your attention on pleasant things as they occur throughout your everyday life. This might include great weather, smooth traffic, green lights, and great parking spaces. These are all beyond our control yet contribute positively to our lives when they occur. When others are kind and helpful, acknowledge how that makes you feel and let them know they made a difference in your day. Shared pleasure makes the world go round.

3. Emphasize the positive. You can be a welcome carrier to a point where people want to spend time with you instead of avoiding you because of your negativity.

4. Listen to ideas shared by others and give credit where it's due. Once stretched by new ideas, the mind cannot retract. Mental expansion is a great way to overcome challenges.

5. Focus on small victories as well as major ones. Celebrate everything! Even if the celebration is nothing more than a "high five," it feels good, doesn't it? Besides, little victories win wars.

6. Practice handling rejection. If anything can get you down, it's constant rejection. Don't take it personally and wallow in it. Learn from it, for it doesn't have to be permanent. Turn the tables on how you think about it, like Tom Hopkins did. He saw each rejection as bringing him closer to that win that he wanted. He used the odds in his favor.

7. Control your frustration before it leads to anger. When feeling frustrated, learn to pause. Take a deep breath or three—or six. Take however many it takes to start to calm down. You can also try counting to ten or even one hundred if you need it to calm yourself so you can think of the most pragmatic way to respond to the situation. Creating space to *respond* instead of *reacting* is the name of the game.

8. Enter every day with purpose. However small, we all must aspire to accomplish at least one thing a day. We must have a reason or goal that can give us the motivation to achieve whatever we set our minds to. It is the simple meaning of life. Little victories lead to success.

9. Compartmentalize. Set time blocks for working on your goals. Proactively put yourself in a positive mindset when working on them. Allocate certain time periods to accomplish business goals and others for personal goals. It's also vital to set special times to

allow yourself to relax. Working and thinking of your problems twenty-four-seven brings into effect the law of diminishing returns. Don't risk becoming ineffective because of mental fatigue. Compartmentalizing helps establish routines for switching gears to other important aspects of your life.

10. Laugh. A good laugh is cathartic. When you need a boost or a change of mood, watch a funny movie or the latest YouTube video from a favorite comedian. Call up that friend who can always make you laugh. Let the lighthearted experiences of others wash over you.

11. Meditate. There are times when we need to just "turn off" or hit the reset button to remove those negative weeds from our minds. Step away from whatever is causing you the most frustration, whether it's a situation or a person. Find a quiet spot to relax, close your eyes, and visualize your happy place. Even doing this for five minutes will leave you refreshed and ready to face what's next.

12. Breathe. Pay attention to your breath. Mentally count the seconds as you breathe in and out. Purposefully slow down your breathing, taking longer to inhale and exhale. Pause, holding your breath at the top of the inhale and at the bottom of your exhale. Taking in more oxygen makes a positive impact on your brain and lessens the stress you feel in your body.

There are always things popping up to throw us off balance and into a depressed state. Even an overloaded to-do list can take you down. Keep a running list, yes, and select one item at a time to focus on productively. A productive mind does a better job of remaining positive, allowing space to tackle whatever opportunities come your way.

If things do get out of control and you feel yourself becoming depressed, seek help. Our minds are our greatest asset. Do whatever it takes to keep your attitude positive so you can operate at maximum capacity.

Lessons Learned:

- It's normal to fall into a negative attitude. Just don't allow yourself to live there.
- No matter what happens, you can choose your attitude in response to the situation.
- Seek out strategies that enhance a positive attitude.

Chapter 21

PRESENTATION

"Everything has beauty but not everyone sees it."
—Confucius

You have to look and act successful in order to be successful. First impressions are extremely important. A positive impression sets the table for what is to come. What impression are you projecting to the world? Take a critical look in the mirror every morning and make changes if you decide you are not projecting the image you want others to see.

Early in my career, my associates and I all took great pride in our appearances. There were no "casual Fridays." San Francisco was a high-end town, and it was important to project a well-put-together image when getting in front of potential employers, clients, and associates. While working in San Francisco, I wore either a suit or an open shirt and a sports coat with dress slacks. We always paid attention to our accessories, such as watches, belts, cuff links, and shoes. The key was to project an image of success.

When things turned for the worse and I hit rock bottom, I did not care about any of that. One reason was that none of my clothes fit any longer. My expensive wardrobe was useless. While working my way back, this was another reason to lose weight and get back in shape. Fitting into my suits was one of many small victories on my path back to success. It was important to get my mojo back if I was going to go out into the world and raise capital. "Looking the part" was the only way to have anyone trust someone like me who had undergone a major loss. It was imperative to look my best and to exude the self-confidence I was slowly re-building within myself.

I had many experiences over the years where I recognized the negative impact appearances had on outcomes. For example, I had the opportunity to interview many people seeking jobs with the various companies I worked with or ran. I could not believe how some people came into the interviews. It was obvious they didn't take pride in their appearance. My thought was this: "If they cannot take care of themselves, then how are they going to be able to take care of our business?" Their visual appearance overrode any confidence they displayed in our interactions.

On the other hand, I recall one impressionable young man's interview. He was well-dressed and started the interview by saying, "You're going to regret it if you don't hire me. This is what I can bring to the table for your company." He then went on, with great energy, to tell me of his experience and skills. He displayed total positive energy and self-confidence. I was impressed, to say the least. And he was right; I did not regret hiring him.

Both visual and verbal positivity come through to others as confidence. Knowledge reinforces confidence. Combine the two, and what you present to the world will be contagious, bringing you greater success when applying for jobs, building relationships, and earning the right to new opportunities.

In real estate, it is vital to present yourself to clients in the most professional manner, even before they look at properties. It's not just about outward appearances but the knowledge we have to share. When real estate is your business, it is critical to study the market in detail to be able to answer questions clients will have. We must exude confidence in our skills and our knowledge of the market.

It's no different for the property. We constantly preach the fact that the outside of a house is more important than the inside. When a person drives up to a home and sees a well-groomed landscape and a well-maintained exterior, it provokes an immediate positive reaction. As they walk through the door, they seek to reinforce that initial impression. They're looking for more positives right from the beginning, so much so that they might even overlook a few negatives. If they drive up to the house and the exterior isn't presentable, they may not even bother going in. They will just drive right on by.

Before I started building apartments in Flagstaff, I went around checking all the other properties in the area to investigate the competition. In one of the first properties I entered, there was a young lady sitting at a desk reading a book. When I walked up to her desk, she looked up at me and said, "Yeah?" I thought to myself, "Are you serious? You have a multimillion-dollar property, and you hire someone who greets people in that manner?" I knew right then and there that I would train my people to project a positive, welcoming, and happy demeanor to prospective tenants as they walked through the door. Every time a potential renter entered our office, they were to be greeted by someone standing up, facing them, and saying, "Welcome to your new home. My name is ___." Our rental rate was always high because we projected the best image possible throughout our properties.

When meeting new people, welcome them with a smile and a gracious greeting while looking the best you can. It is extremely difficult to overturn a negative first impression. It's also difficult to ruin a good one. Your appearance is a billboard announcing to everyone, "This is who I am!" Dress according to the audience you are trying to attract into your sphere of influence. My friend, Tom Hopkins, suggests dressing like a person others would go to for advice.

Depending on the type of people you want to get involved with, this may mean dressing one step up or several. Analyze your current wardrobe and decide if it needs upgrading. If it does, set goals for acquiring good-quality clothing a few pieces at a time. Keep your wardrobe simple, well-fitting, and clean. Wear what you believe best demonstrates your individuality and what you believe is appropriate pertaining to the circumstances. Avoid outrageous extremes in either direction.

My Italian grandfather always wore a suit, even when he was not working. He would tell me that you could never be overdressed. You can be underdressed, but you will never feel out of place if you are overdressed. People will notice and make comments about how nice you look. Always try to put your best foot forward. When you look the part, you will feel the part, and your energy will show that.

Hygiene is also mandatory. I cannot stress the importance of health and hygiene to your mental well-being. The exterior body also needs to be taken care of and well-maintained. This completes the total you. Cleanliness is imperative. If you are ungroomed or have poor hygiene standards, people will want to get as far away from you as possible.

Projecting a positive, healthy, and confident image is not difficult. It only requires that you pay attention to that projection and make any adjustments necessary each and every day.

Lessons Learned:

- Whether we like it or not, your physical appearance makes an impression that can determine whether or not you get access to new opportunities.
- Dressing the part of whatever role you want is a crucial element in gaining interest, building trust, and generating confidence.
- The person you see in the mirror must demonstrate the attitude and competence you desire to put forth into the world.
- Convey success in a humble manner.

Chapter 22

PARTICIPATION

"Friends show their love in times of trouble, not in happiness. Life has no blessing like a prudent friend."
—Euripides

There are blue zones around the world, areas where people live the longest and are the healthiest. Often living past one hundred years old, most of these people state that involvement in their communities is the key ingredient to their health and longevity. They are extremely social, communing both with nature and with the other people living near them. I can't overemphasize the importance of this aspect for living a fulfilling life.

Most opportunities to succeed in life require interactions with others. It is through our human connections that we learn communication skills that allow us to project ourselves as valuable world citizens, partners, and associates. Developing a network of friends and associates is critical to long-term success and happiness.

To develop strong relationships, make a concerted effort to be present when you are with others. I am constantly amazed when I walk into restaurants to see small groups of people having dinner, yet several of them are looking at something on their phones. Isn't the whole point of having dinner with someone to interact with them? We have become addicted to social media in such a way that we have developed a culture of zombies—and these zombies have no personal social skills whatsoever! I believe there are few things in the world as satisfying as sharing a meal and a great conversation with another person, whether the topic is current events, a new opportunity, or something personal.

Believe me, I'm not saying to turn off your phones and stay off the internet. What I am saying is there is a time and place for you to be directly engaged with the living, breathing people in front of you. When you're with people, interact with them, get to know them, and be pleasant. Have a conversation, and work on your social skills. If you're glued to the internet all day long, how can you feel comfortable when you're sitting directly in front of another person? Comfort only comes through deliberate practice.

A good way to meet new people is to join social groups with a common interest. For example, if you like to read, you could visit the numerous book clubs that seem to meet regularly in every area. Not only do you find interesting people in these groups, but you learn from reading interesting material. There are also walking clubs, bike clubs, running clubs, bridge clubs, domino clubs, and so on, just to name a few.

A common course of treatment for depression is to get out and do something beneficial for others. This worked quite well for me during my dark times. I chose to volunteer for charity organizations. I was struggling to fill all the hours in my day, so I went to the local food bank to offer my help. These organizations are constantly looking for volunteers to help service less fortunate individuals. You would be surprised by the number of interesting people you meet within the volunteer service. You will meet people who are more concerned for others than themselves. These are the types of compassionate friends you want in your life.

Working as a volunteer also provides you with a sense of self-satisfaction. My time volunteering made me feel better because I was providing value, and it took my mind off of my problems. I could not help but leave each volunteer shift in a positive state. It also provided me with additional motivation to recover from my own challenges. When I realized the fate of others, I knew I didn't want to follow the same path. I highly encourage you to participate in volunteering your time to others. No matter how unhappy or depressed you are, helping others will help bring you out of that funk.

After numerous volunteer shifts, I started to meet the people behind one particular organization that provided meals to the homeless, called Andrea House. Eventually, I was asked to join their Board of Directors. This allowed me to meet many influential individuals who were not only on the Board but also involved in sponsoring events. These connections helped me expand my network with even more like-minded individuals. While my volunteer work was not intended to benefit me personally, it ended up doing so through the connections I made.

Through my volunteer work, I learned that being friendly and putting a smile on your face puts you in a happy place. Not only are you exuding positive energy, but you feel better about yourself. As you go out in public with that smile, you will find that it is quite easy to talk to other people. Typically, they will appreciate the opportunity to get to know a happy person.

In all interactions, practice the art of conversation. You don't have to say anything thing about yourself to make an excellent impression. Show interest in others instead. Ask questions about them and let them know you are interested in what they have to say. You may gain great insight from their life experiences. I guarantee you will make a positive impression and walk away with that individual thinking about what a wonderful person you are.

Also, work on developing deeper personal friendships. Stay in touch regularly with friends and associates. Not every connection needs to be about a deal or opportunity. Caring for others is rewarding in so many ways. My efforts to maintain my lifelong friendships have come back to benefit me abundantly. My best friends were always there to give me a helping hand, and I did the same for them. I firmly believe that you must give before you can receive. As you look back on my story, please understand that every positive opportunity was presented to me by an individual I met along the way and the relationship I worked to develop. These contacts helped me become who I am. Meet people, for they are the guiding light to a positive future.

Lessons Learned:

- Developing a network of friends and reliable associates is critical to overcoming challenges and creating new opportunities.
- Lending a helping hand to others, even with the simplest skills you have, brings satisfaction and potentially great rewards.
- Practice the art of conversation with a sincere interest in others.

Chapter 23

YOUR SELF LOVE

"He whom love touches
does not walk in darkness."
—Plato

We are in control of our health, attitudes, projections, and participation—the topics we covered in the previous four chapters. We all have the ability to improve ourselves, both physically and in how we present ourselves to the world. All we need to do is consistently make the best choices we can to live the life of our dreams.

In this chapter, I want to help you realize that you already hold the keys to that better life. In fact, no one else can create it for you. You are the creator of your reality. I hope that doesn't shock you. Rather, I ask you to be honest with yourself. Take a look around you. Think about where you are in life, including where you are living and who you spend time with. Those are the results of the choices you have made.

While choosing to embrace a new and improved positive approach to your life, it is imperative that you begin by loving who you are. No more beating yourself up. No more dwelling on past mistakes. Accept who you are today *and* who you are dedicated to becoming. Love yourself!

You see, when we do not love ourselves, or even if we simply dislike ourselves and the choices we've made, we set ourselves up for hard times, challenges, failure, and defeat. If *we* don't like ourselves, how could we possibly expect others to? Having a healthy love of self is foundational to every level of success in our lives.

You might be wondering, "But how do I create that "healthy love of self?" Well, your ability to love yourself depends on how you spend your time.

During my college years, I took a course in psychology. It made such a major impact on me that I can still recall the key points of the course. The main message was to never underthink the value of time. We are all born with the gift of time, though we never know how much. Time is the most precious part of our lives, and until we realize that, we tend to waste and squander it. Yet, our psychological well-being is measured by how we allocate our time.

In this course, there were three elements for measuring time. The first element is "a means to an end." That type of time describes doing something you don't enjoy or look forward to. For instance, if you hate your job or you don't like going to school, these activities would be defined as a means to an end.

The second element is "fun time." This describes instances when you are simply enjoying yourself and you have no concept of time. This might be time spent on vacation or just hanging out with friends. We all enjoy experiencing this element when it happens.

The third element of how we spend our time is "emotional." Essentially, this is referencing time spent in an emotional state, such as anger, worry, sadness, fear, or love. This sense of time often focuses on negativity, and I have given you tools to remove as much of that type of time as possible from your daily routine. However, sometimes we just can't help it, and we find ourselves in an emotional state of mind, and it takes everything we have to escape it. An example of this would be time spent facing the loss of a loved one or a tremendous failure in a business situation. The goal, of course, is to spend the majority of our time focusing on positive emotions, but this is not always realistic. In the case where negative emotions are unavoidable, I'm not telling you to deny your feelings. Feel them, but love yourself enough to avoid dwelling on the negative ones for long.

How often we participate in each of these time elements dictates our sense of balance. Interestingly, we tend to align ourselves with others who are operating in the same time element that we are. Fun likes to have a good time and play. When that's where your time focus is, it's very unlikely that you're going to enjoy being around someone who is in the "means to an end" frame of mind. When you are ready to spend time in productive work, the "fun time" associates will not be so much fun. When you are experiencing negative emotions, it's highly unlikely that you will attract others into your world who are experiencing positive emotions A well-balanced individual maintains equilibrium within themselves, fostering a sense of comfort. However, not every individual possesses the same balance ratio. It is imperative that whoever blends into your life shares a similar balance or is comfortable with your ratio, allowing you to be your authentic self.

To better illustrate this, let's say our relationships resemble an atom. Each atom consists of a nucleus, protons, and electrons. Protons represent positive energy, while electrons represent negative energy. Similar to an atom attracting more protons and electrons into its orbit to form a stronger element, life follows a similar pattern. As we cultivate more positive energy within ourselves to navigate the negativity encountered in our daily lives, we, like the atom, become stronger.

This is similar to how humans function in that we all have positive and negative energy circulating around us. We all seek to have a strong balance, as does each atom.

As people (and atoms) blend with one another, they can only become stronger. Now, you ask, what does this have to do with loving yourself? This analogy symbolizes how we attract others into our sphere.

Imagine each of us as a nucleus and the people around us as protons and electrons. The effect others have on us reflects our inner strength and the balance we have created in our lives. We, as the nucleus of our lives, must learn to love and appreciate who we are first. The stronger the nucleus, the stronger the balance.

As we go through life consciously putting ourselves in a state of positive energy, we become the nucleus that attracts people who support the life, strength, and situations we desire. We can only do that as long as we believe in ourselves, love ourselves, and remain dedicated to balance.

Once we can establish balance within ourselves and understand and love who we are, we can then go out into the world and seek relationships that will enhance our lives. We cannot make anyone love us. However, we can decide how much and how well we love ourselves. When we love ourselves well, we convey a positive self-worth that will attract others. This is the first step toward developing loving relationships.

I believe we all need love in our lives. Whether that love comes from another person, a spiritual entity, or an animal. That sense of love that comes from beyond us is so satisfying. If you are fortunate to have love in your life with another person, know that you are blessed. Keeping a loving relationship alive takes work by both parties as they must love themselves, project a positive attitude, and participate in the relationship.

It is wonderful to know that you are not facing the world alone. Knowing there is another person who cares about you is important to all of us. I suffered through many difficult breakups, but I was never discouraged enough to permanently give up on having a solid, rewarding, and loving relationship in my life. I guess I have always been a romantic at heart.

A lot of people are seeking love and are frustrated because the harder they look, the more difficult it seems to find. When you maintain an upbeat, positive energy within your expanding social circle, you may be surprised how love might come to you when you least expect it. Notice that it starts with your positive energy and self-love.

If you have had challenging relationships or even a recent loss, know that there are still opportunities to have great love in your life. When I was at rock bottom, I met the person whose love has benefited my life the most. I had little to offer other than my positive belief that my life would get better. It was my ability to emanate that positive energy even during tough times that allowed me to attract and pursue that relationship. I now spend my days loving the one person who helps me build a better life day by day.

Lessons Learned:

- Self-love is more important than any other kind.
- Strive to balance the time life has given you.
- Staying open to opportunities for great love is vital.
- Every day we are here has the possibility to bring on a new opportunity. Always be prepared to seize the moment.

AFTERWORD

The titles of the last five chapters of this book were chosen for a specific purpose. By using the first letter of each title, you spell HAPPY. I truly believe that following the practices in those five chapters led to my current happiness in life. The advice in those chapters was derived from the lessons I learned during my wins and losses.

Throughout these pages, my goal was to help you establish a strong emotional connection with your inner self. To overcome the fear of failure and loss of self-confidence, one must look for inner strength and set aside whatever negative emotions were created by loss. Continually develop a strong sense of self-worth and self-confidence that will enable you to proceed through life with a positive attitude.

Some people accomplish this by posting positive notes of encouragement around their homes as a reminder to stay positive and motivated. Others encourage themselves with inner pep talks to promote positivity. A lot of people enjoy reading motivational books. Whatever works for you, do it; remember, it is a continuous effort on your part. You cannot let your mind "slack off," so to speak. If you get lazy in your motivation, the result will not be very rewarding.

Once you have established your inner and outer self, you will exude the positive energy and confidence necessary to interact with others, and in that process, you might even find love. This, I believe, is what leads to a successful and happy life. Positivity is infectious, and people will want to be around when you exude a positive aura. This aura will attract others to you, which can lead to incredible opportunities and loving relationships.

Without an attitude of positivity, it's easy to experience an emptiness within yourself. When you dwell in negativity, you feel you are going nowhere. Unfortunately, most people with this attitude don't understand why they are so unhappy.

It took losing everything I had to understand who I really was. I had put so much importance on *things* I had acquired rather than on my inner being. I believed my self-worth was my net worth. I was wrong in so many ways. I believe this thought process had a lot to do with my upbringing. Going out into the world with a poor farmer mentality was tough. I was completely insecure and had a huge inferiority complex. After all my successes, the pendulum swung to the other side, and I was not a very nice person. My newfound ego got in the way. I had to start over to understand who I really was and who I wanted to be. I acquired a level of humility that was previously non-existent. I realized every person has something to offer. Interactions with others aren't just about what they can do for me. I now understand my inner self and who I really am. This has probably been the most rewarding experience of all: knowing that people could like me for who I am, not what I have.

I believe true happiness means being happy with who you are and enjoying the company of others. The human mind is the most powerful organ we have, so use it. Go out into the ever-changing world and be the best, most positive winner you can be. As I stated earlier, happiness is the journey, not the destination. This big, beautiful world we live in is a gift, and it is up to each and every one of us to take advantage of this gift by being the best we can be and enjoying everything we are offered. We are all winners by just being here and doing our best to remain positive.

"Success is determined not by the completion of some action, but by how one engages in all action with wisdom and intelligence."—Plato.

ACKNOWLEDGMENTS

I acknowledge my family and loved ones for their encouragement to write the story of my crazy roller coaster of a life. My great appreciation goes to my two editors, Janine Hernandez and Judy Slack, for guiding me through this process from start to finish and the Made For Success publishing team for getting me to the finish line. I couldn't have accomplished this without your help.

Great thanks go to my dear friends who were there through thick and thin to lend a helping hand when needed: Bill Dorey, Steve Jones, and Mike Gompertz. I don't know where I'd be today if I didn't have you in my life.

My dear friend, Tom Hopkins, inspired me along the way to put my thoughts in writing and helped with his suggestions. I thank my two sons, Rob and Mike, for badgering me into putting my thoughts and experiences down on paper and never quitting, even when I had doubts.

Last but never least, I want to acknowledge Debra Richardson, my special partner, for always listening and guiding me through these golden chapters.

ABOUT THE AUTHOR

Robert Banovac is a man of diverse experiences and unwavering determination. He holds a Bachelor of Science in Chemistry with a minor in business and pursued an MBA until he received a draft notice, showcasing his commitment to duty. Inspired by his life stories, his two sons encouraged him to write a book, aiming to pass on his legacy and inspire others to never give up. Robert's involvement in philanthropy as a past board member for Helping Hands Non-Profit (later merged with UMOM) exemplifies his compassionate nature. In his leisure time, Robert enjoys old movies, walks on the beach, the occasional round of golf, and having dinner with his family and friends. He enjoys heading to the gym for a workout. He loves to travel and find a beach to enjoy the ocean. Robert splits his time between Phoenix and Mexico, relishing the best of both worlds.

BIBLIOGRAPHY

(2020, November 13). Socrates advice to married people. Greece High Definition. https://www.greecehighdefinition .com/blog/2020/11/13/socrates-married-people-marriage -xanthippe.

"Heraclitus Quotes." *Quotes.net.* STANDS4 LLC, 2023. Web. 4 Oct. 2023. <https://www.quotes.net/quote/57226>.

"Plato Quotes." Quotes.net. STANDS$LLC, 2023. Web. 4 Oct. 2023. https://www.quptes.net/quote/49981.

Borghini, A. (2019, July 25). Quotes about friendships from some of the greatest thinkers of time. Thought Co. https://www .thoughtco.com/best-friendship-quotes-2670520.

Bryan, V. (2013, July 17) Heraclitus (535-475BCE) Classical Wisdom. https://classicalwisdom.com/people/philosophers /heraclitus-535-475-bce/#:~:text=By%20this%20he%20 means%20that,the%20river%20is%20changed%20 permanently.

Chapman, J. (2018, February 21). What you do is who you become. Medium. https://medium.com/performance-course /what-you-do-is-who-you-become-388aedfd896f.

Confucius Quotes. (n.d.). BrainyQuote.com. Retrieved October 4,2023, from BrainyQuote.com Web site: https://www.brainy quote.com/quotes/confucius_104254.

Confucius. The Analects of Confucius: A Philosophical Translation. New York: Ballantine Books, 1999.

Epicurus Quotes. (n.d.). BrainyQuote.com. Retrieved October 4, 2023, from BrainyQuote.com Web site: https://www.brainy quote.com/quotes/epicurus_133089.

Feel Joy. (2018, October 1). Life is simple but we insist on making it complicated. Medium. https://feeljoy.medium .com/life-is-simple-but-we-insist-on-making-it-complicated -c1e910a13431.

Hypatia. Ecsite. https://www.ecsite.eu/activities-and-services /projects/Hypatia.

Jackson, R. (2012, October 18). The 25 biggest regrets in life. What are yours? Forbes. https://www.forbes.com/sites/eric jackson/2012/10/18/the-25-biggest-regrets-in-life-what-are -yours/?sh=1a1b63576488.

Lavinsky, D. (2023). Calvin Coolidge was almost right. Growthink. https://www.growthink.com/content/calvin -coolidge-was-almost-right.

Mackay, H. (2023, May). There are no negatives to keeping a positive attitude. Harvey Mackay Academy. https:// harveymackayacademy.com/there-are-no-negatives-to-keeping -a-positive-attitude/.

Maxfield, C. (2016, June 4). What we achieve inwardly will change outer reality. Clarie Maxfield. https://claremaxfield .com.au/2087-2/.

Meadows, D. (2009, January 16) Herophilus Quote. Rogue Classicism. https://rogueclassicism.com/2009/01/16/hero philus-quote/.

Plato (2012). "Symposium and Phaedrus," p.29, Courier Corporation.

Plato, Apology 22d, translated by Harold North Fowler, 1966.

Singh, R. (2021, February 17). 6 Lessons from the 'founder' of McDonalds. My Story. https://yourstory.com/mystory /3c67120cab-6-lessons-from-the-founder-of-mcdonald-s.

Sofield, D. (2017, October 21). It's not what happens to you, but how you react to it that matters. Medium. https://medium .com/@debsofield/its-not-what-happens-to-you-but-how-you -react-to-it-that-matters-73808376ee0c.

Sonshi. (1999). Sun Tzu's Art of War Original Translation by Sonshi. https://www.sonshi.com/sun-tzu-art-of-war -translation-original.html.

Team Soul (2018, September 19). It is during our darkest moments that we must focus to see the light. https://iam fearlesssoul.com/it-is-during-our-darkest-moments-that-we -must-focus-to-see-the-light/.

The Art of Living: The Classic Manual on Virtue, Happiness, and Effectiveness, A New Interpretation by Sharon Lebell." Book by Epictetus, 1994.

The Eagles, "Desperado." Desperado. https://genius.com /Eagles-desperado-lyrics.

The Trix. (2019, November 25). Happiness resides not in possessions, not in gold, happiness resides in the soul. Medium. https://medium.com/afwp/happiness-resides-not -in-possessions-and-not-in-gold-happiness-dwells-in-the -soul-d49fa65d4a5e#:~:text=Few%20Words%20%7C%20 Medium-,%E2%80%9CHappiness%20resides%20 not%20in%20possessions%2C%20and%20not%20 in%20gold%2C,happiness%20dwells%20in%20the%20 soul%E2%80%9D&text=This%20quote%20from%20 Democritus%20is,as%20a%20value%20for%20happiness.